# USBORNE
# ACTIVITIES
## FOR ALL YEAR ROUND

### Angela Wilkes

Edited by Felicity Brooks

Designed by
Andrea Slane and Sarah Sherley-Price

Cover and additional designs by Zöe Wray

Managing Editor: Felicity Brooks
Managing Designer: Stephen Wright
Still life photography: Howard Allman and
Amanda Heywood
Decorative borders by Kate Mawdsley
Design assistant: Katarina Dragoslavić
Photographic manipulation: John Russell
Meteorology consultant: Francis Wilson
Astronomy consultant: Stuart Atkinson
American editor: Carrie Seay

Illustrated by Dave Ashby, John Barber, Amanda Barlow, Andrew Beckett, Joyce Bee, Stephen Bennett, Roland Berry, Gary Bines, Isabel Bowring, Trevor Boyer, Peter Bull, Hilary Burn, Lynn Chadwick, Christine Darter, David Eaton, Denise Finney, John Francis, Don Forrest, Victoria Gordon, Teri Gower, Prue Greener, David Hancock, Tim Hayward, Christine Howe, Chris Howell-Jones, David Hurrell, Ian Jackson, Roger Kent, Aziz Khan, Kim Lane, Jonathan Langley, Richard Lewington, Kevin Lyles, Josephine Martin, Malcolm McGregor, Doreen McGuinness, Annabel Milne, Barbara Nicholson, Richard Orr, Lucy Parris, Julie Piper, Maurice Pledger, Charles Raymond, Phillip Richardson, Mike Rickets, Jim Robins, John Russell, Chris Shields, Peter Stebbing, Sue Stitt, Justine Torode, David Watson, Phil Weare, Adrian Williams, Roy Wiltshire, John Woodcock, David Wright, John Yates, Norman Young

# Contents

# The changing seasons

In most parts of the world, the seasons change throughout the year. There are four seasons: spring, summer, fall and winter and they follow each other in the same pattern every year. Each season is different. The weather changes and the days grow longer or shorter. In this book you can find out which special things to look for in each season and ideas on things to make or do.

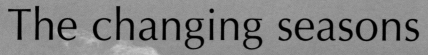

## Spring

In spring the weather becomes warmer and the days grow longer. The first flowers appear and trees burst into leaf and blossom. Spring is also the time when most birds build their nests and many animals have babies.

## Summer

Summer is the warmest season of the year. The days are long and sunny and the nights are short. The trees are green and leafy and there are lots of flowers, fruit and vegetables. Animals and insects are all busy looking for food.

Baby animals, such as this Black tail deer, are born in the spring so they have time to grow strong before winter comes again.

In the summer, bees and butterflies fly from flower to flower in search of nectar.

The leaves of some trees turn yellow, red and orange in the fall.

## Fall

In the fall, the days grow shorter and the nights longer. It is cooler than in summer. Many trees change color, then lose their leaves. Animals get ready for the winter ahead, stocking up on food or settling down for a long sleep.

## Winter

Winter is the coldest time of year. The days are short and the nights are long. Many places have snow and frost. Many trees are bare and there are very few flowers or insects around. Some animals sleep all winter long.

When it is very cold in the winter, trees are sometimes covered in a silvery coating of frost.

# Skywatching

On a clear night the sky is full of stars. They look close together but they are millions of miles apart. Long ago, people noticed that the stars formed patterns or constellations in the night sky.

## Star charts

Because the Earth is always moving around the Sun, we see different constellations from month to month. In this book you will find star charts for each season of the year, showing the main constellations to look for.

Pegasus

Andromeda

Cassiopeia

To make it easier to recognize the constellations, people gave them names and made up stories about them.

Perseus

You may sometimes see a meteor or shooting star.

The white band on each map shows a faint band of stars. This is the Milky Way.

People in the southern half of the world see different stars from people in the northern half because they are looking at a different part of the sky. This is why you will find four charts for every season. Find the right star charts for where you live and follow the instructions.

## Constellations

The lines joining the stars show the constellation. This is the constellation of Ursa Major, or the Great Bear. The imaginary shape of a bear is drawn around the constellation to show why it got its name.

The seven stars at the back of the bear, shown here in yellow, are also known as the Big Dipper.

## Seeing farther

You can see a lot farther into space if you use binoculars. You can pick out the planets, spot craters on the Moon and you may even see a comet.

Astronomers use telescopes to see thousands of times farther into space.

Binoculars

Stars seen with the naked eye

The same stars seen through binoculars

The same stars seen through a good telescope

# Why are there seasons?

The Earth is constantly spinning around the Sun. It takes a year to go around the Sun once. However, the Earth is not upright as it spins, but tilted slightly to one side. This means that whichever part of the Earth is tilting toward the Sun gets more sunlight. Because the Earth is moving, different parts tilt toward the Sun at different times of year. This makes the seasons change.

In March, neither the northern nor southern half of the Earth tilts toward the Sun. It's spring in the north and fall in the south.

In December and January the southern half of the Earth tilts toward the Sun, so it's summer there.

It's winter in the northern half in December and January because it is tilting away from the Sun.

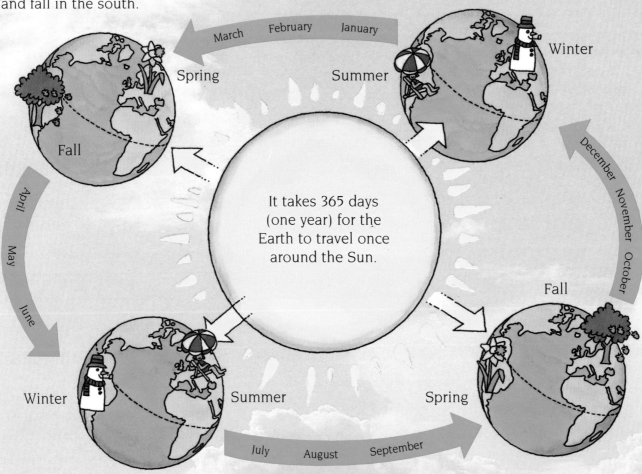

March February January

Spring

Summer

Winter

April

May

June

December November October

Fall

It takes 365 days (one year) for the Earth to travel once around the Sun.

Fall

Winter

Summer

Spring

July August September

In June, it's winter in the southern half of the Earth because it is tilting away from the Sun. It's summer in the northern half.

The area around the middle of the Earth has about the same amount of sunlight all year, so the seasons don't change much.

In September, neither the northern nor the southern half is tilting toward the Sun. It is fall in the north and spring in the south.

# Spring

# The spring sky at night

These star maps will help you identify the constellations that you can see in the night sky in spring. The best time to use the maps is at around 11pm on a clear night, away from city lights.

## Maps for northern half of world

The maps on this page show the stars that people in the northern half of the world can see, looking north and looking south. The names of the constellations are shown in capital letters. The only star in the sky that doesn't seem to change its position is the Pole Star, in the middle of the top map.

Look for the famous constellation Ursa Major (the Great Bear) overhead.

Regulus shines in the middle of the sky. It is part of the constellation of Leo (the Lion).

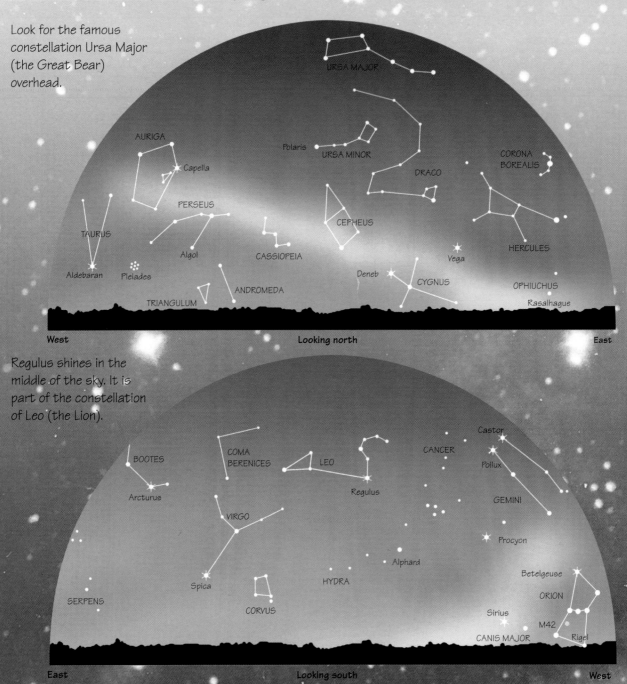

URSA MAJOR

AURIGA

Capella

Polaris

URSA MINOR

CORONA BOREALIS

DRACO

PERSEUS

CEPHEUS

TAURUS

Algol

CASSIOPEIA

HERCULES

Vega

Aldebaran   Pleiades

Deneb

CYGNUS

OPHIUCHUS

ANDROMEDA

Rasalhague

TRIANGULUM

**West**                          Looking north                          **East**

BOOTES

COMA BERENICES

LEO

CANCER

Castor

Pollux

Arcturus

Regulus

GEMINI

VIRGO

Procyon

Alphard

Betelgeuse

Spica

HYDRA

ORION

SERPENS

CORVUS

Sirius

M42

Rigel

CANIS MAJOR

**East**                          Looking south                          **West**

# Maps for southern half of world

These maps show the stars that people in the southern half of the world can see in spring. Facing north, the constellations of Pegasus and Andromeda dominate the sky. The ruby red star Aldebaran shines brightly in the east.

The most famous constellation in the skies of the southern half of the world is Crux, known as the Southern Cross. You cannot see it from the northern half of the world at any time of the year.

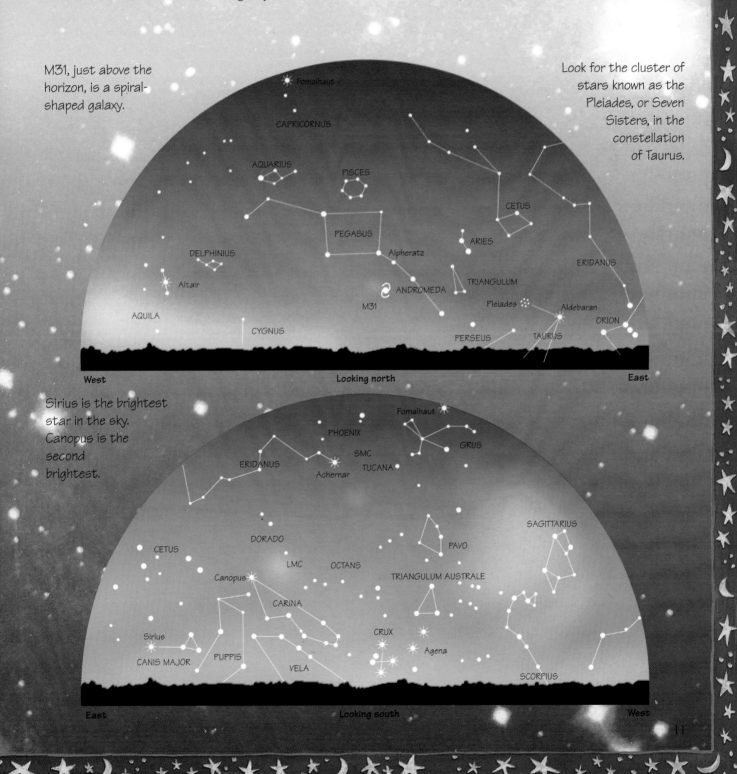

M31, just above the horizon, is a spiral-shaped galaxy.

Look for the cluster of stars known as the Pleiades, or Seven Sisters, in the constellation of Taurus.

Fomalhaut

CAPRICORNUS

AQUARIUS

PISCES

CETUS

PEGASUS

ARIES

DELPHINIUS

Alpheratz

ERIDANUS

Altair

TRIANGULUM

ANDROMEDA

AQUILA

M31

Pleiades

Aldebaran

ORION

CYGNUS

PERSEUS

TAURUS

**West**          **Looking north**          **East**

Sirius is the brightest star in the sky. Canopus is the second brightest.

Fomalhaut

PHOENIX

GRUS

SMC

ERIDANUS

TUCANA

Achernar

SAGITTARIUS

DORADO

PAVO

CETUS

LMC          OCTANS

TRIANGULUM AUSTRALE

Canopus

CARINA

CRUX

Sirius

Agena

CANIS MAJOR          PUPPIS

VELA

SCORPIUS

**East**          **Looking south**          **West**

11

# Weatherwatch

In spring, the weather can change very quickly. Strong winds and sudden showers are often followed by rainbows or sunshine.

You can find out how strong the wind is by looking out for signs around you. Watching the clouds can also give you clues as to what kind of weather is on the way.

## Rainbows

If the sun comes out between clouds when it is raining, it shines through the drops of water and you may suddenly see a rainbow. Rainbows are always on the opposite side of the sky from the sun, so you have to stand with your back to the sun to see them. The colors in a rainbow are always in the same order – red, orange, yellow, green, blue, indigo and violet.

*Red is always the color at the top or outside of a rainbow. Violet is always at the bottom, or inside of it.*

## Wind speed

Weather forecasters use instruments to measure wind speed. You can estimate it by looking for the following signs.

Calm. Smoke from chimneys rises straight up. 0-2mph.

Light breeze. Smoke shows wind direction. Wind felt on face. 4-7mph.

Fresh breeze. Small waves on lakes. Small trees sway. 19-24mph.

Strong breeze. Hard to hold umbrellas. Big branches move. 25-31mph.

Gale. Difficult to walk. Small branches broken off trees. 39-46mph.

Storm. Trees uprooted and buildings damaged. 55-63mph.

# Cloud spotting

Clouds are made of millions of tiny drops of water. If you watch them for a while, you will see they are constantly changing shape and size. New clouds sometimes appear out of blue sky and vanish again just as quickly. Some clouds are a sign of good weather. Others show that the weather is about to change and rain is on its way.

Tall, dark cumulonimbus clouds with flat tops may bring rain and thunderstorms.

A thick layer of nimbostratus clouds blocks the sun and makes it a dull day.

Altostratus clouds form a patchy sheet of clouds that the sun can filter through.

Wispy cirrus clouds high in the sky show that wind and rain may be coming.

Large, fluffy, white cumulus clouds are usually seen on fine, sunny days.

Cirrostratus clouds form a thin film across the sky. They often bring rain.

Palm trees blowing in storm-force winds

Stratus clouds form a low layer across the sky. They can bring light rain and drizzle.

Altocumulus are small clouds all about the same size. They often lie in rows.

# Spring landscape

As the weather gets warmer, you could try painting a spring landscape. Watercolors are good for painting skies and water, especially if you paint your picture on wet paper so that the colors run together. It is best to paint the picture in two stages, letting the colors dry in between.

## You will need
Watercolor paints
Thick and fine paintbrushes
A small sponge
Watercolor paper
A plate or palette

## Painting a wash

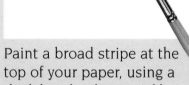

Paint a broad stripe at the top of your paper, using a thick brush. Then quickly paint more stripes below it.

## Mixing colors

**1.** It is best to mix watercolors on a palette. Wet your brush and dab one color onto your palette.

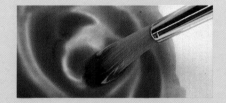

**2.** Rinse the brush, then dip it into another color and mix it into the first color on your palette.

Tulips flower in the spring. Huge fields of them grow in The Netherlands.

# Windmill picture

**1.** Wet the sponge, then use it to wet the bottom half of the watercolor paper.

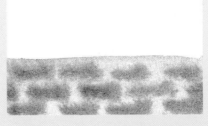

**2.** Brush short strokes of one shade of blue across the wet paper, using a thick brush.

**3.** Do the same with the other blue and the green. Let the colors run together.

**4.** Wet the top of the paper with the sponge. Paint a pale blue wash across it.

**5.** Let the paint dry. Paint a broad green stripe and gray windmill shapes.

**6.** Paint shadows on the windmills. Use a fine brush to paint thin lines for sails.

**7.** Paint green leaves in the foreground of the picture, then paint red tulip flowers above them.

# Roots and shoots

In the spring, new plants start to grow from seeds. You can watch how tiny roots and shoots grow by soaking bean seeds in a glass jar.

Runner beans grow from seeds.

## You will need

A big glass jar
A paper towel or a paper napkin

Bean seeds
Water
A spoon

## What to do

**1.** Soak any labels off the jar, then rinse it out with cold water. You don't need to dry it.

**2.** Fold the paper towel or paper napkin in half. Roll it into a tube and slip it into the jar.

**3.** Press the paper towel against the sides of the jar with the handle of the spoon, as shown.

**4.** Peel back part of the paper. Push one of the bean seeds down between the jar and the paper.

**5.** Push two more beans into the jar. Spoon water onto the paper until it is really wet.

**6.** Stand the jar in a bright, warm place. Water it every day to keep the paper wet. Watch what happens.

The beans swell and the outer skins split. Tiny roots start to grow downward.

Next, small green shoots uncurl and start to grow upward. You can barely see the leaves.

White rootlets grow from the roots and leaves grow.

## Bean plants

Plant the plants in pots or straight in the garden. Tie them to garden sticks and water them regularly. By the end of the summer you will be able to pick your own beans.

The plants on the right are ready to be planted in pots or in a garden.

# Spring daisies

You can create your own everlasting spring flowers by making them out of tissue paper. Make enough for a small bouquet, or arrange them in a vase.

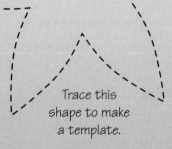

Trace this shape to make a template.

## You will need
White, yellow and green tissue paper
Tracing paper
A pencil
A pin
A paperclip
Scissors
Clear glue
A drinking straw that bends

## Making a daisy

**1.** Trace this daisy onto a piece of tracing paper. Trace the dot in the middle. Then cut out the shape to make a template.

**2.** Cut out 3 squares of white tissue paper 9 x 9cm (4 x 4in). Lay them together and draw around the template.

**3.** Mark the dot with a pin. Remove the template and clip the paper flowers together with the paper clip.

**4.** Cut out the flower shapes. Fold them in half, without creasing them. Snip across the hole in the middle.

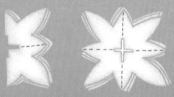

**5.** Unfold the petals. Fold them the other way, then snip across the hole again. Open the petals out flat.

**6.** Cut out a square of yellow tissue 12cm (5in) across. Make a ball of yellow paper and put it on the square.

**7.** Wrap the tissue paper around the ball and twist it. Hold the tail and tap the ball to flatten it.

**8**. Push the tail of the ball through the hole in the daisy petals. Lick your fingers and gently twist the petals to fan them out.

**9.** Cut out some green tissue paper 20 x 5cm (8 x 2in). Glue along one long edge, then roll the straw up in it, starting at the unglued end.

**10.** Dab glue around the yellow base of the daisy, then push it firmly down into one end of the drinking straw flower stem.

Arrange your spring daisies in a colorful vase or wrap them in tissue paper.

# Planting seeds

Plant flower seeds indoors early in spring and they will flower in the summer. Here you can see how to grow pansies from seeds but you can plant most other small flower seeds in the same way. Check the backs of your seed packets for more information.

## You will need

| | |
|---|---|
| The bottom part of an eggbox | Pansy seeds |
| Potting compost | A sieve |
| A spoon | Newspaper |
| | A watering can |
| | Flowerpots |

Pansies have velvety petals.

## What to do

**1.** Rinse the eggbox and let it drip. Half fill each section of the eggbox with potting compost.

**2.** Plant two seeds in each section, with a gap between them. Sift compost on top and press it down.

**3.** Cover the eggbox with newspaper and leave it outside. Water the compost every few days.

**4.** After about two weeks, shoots will appear. Remove the newspaper so they get plenty of light.

**5.** When the shoots have two leaves each, pull out the smaller shoot in each section of the eggbox.

**6.** As the pansies grow bigger, tiny roots will begin to grow through the sides of the eggbox.

**7.** Soak the eggbox in water, then gently pull the sections apart. Half-fill the flowerpots with potting compost.

**8.** Plant a section of the eggbox in each pot. Add more compost and press it down around the plant gently.

## Looking after your pansies

Put the flowerpots outside in a warm, sunny spot and water them whenever the compost looks dry. Pick off dead flowerheads and your pansies should keep flowering all summer long.

*You can plant your pansies in flowerpots or straight in flowerbeds if you like.*

# Pondwatching

Spring is a good time to study ponds and streams because the plants are flowering and lots of small creatures live there. But take an adult with you, stay on the bank and be very careful not to fall in. If you take along a fishing net and some collecting equipment, you can take a closer look at things that live in the water.

If you are lucky, you may see a kingfisher by a pond, diving to catch fish.

## Pond dipping

Here you can see what to look for in a pond. If you have a net, sweep it gently through the water and put its contents in a jar so that you can study them. Put any plants and animals back into the pond as soon as you have looked at them.

### You will need
Clean glass jars
A fishing net with a small mesh
Binoculars
A magnifying glass or hand lens
Empty plastic containers for interesting finds

Look along the banks for flowers, reeds and grasses.

Look among reeds for birds' nests, but do not disturb them.

Water lily

Water lily

Damselfly

Moorhen chick

Look for holes in the banks where animals might live.

Look at the surface of the pond for insects, birds and plants.

Great crested newt

Stickleback

Great diving beetle

Great pond snail

In a stream, look under stones for worms, insects and leeches.

Water shrew

## Looking at newts

Newts look similar to small lizards, but they are smooth instead of scaly. Like frogs and toads, they are amphibians. This means that they are born in water, but spend most of their adult lives on land. In the spring, newts head for water to find a mate and lay their eggs.

A male smooth newt shows off to a female by arching his back and flicking his tail.

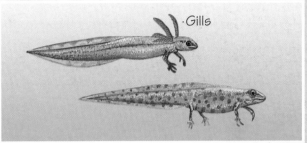

Gills

Newts lay their eggs underwater one at a time, on water plants.

The tadpoles hatch from the eggs after about two weeks.

Newt tadpoles have feathery gills which they use to breathe.

Most of the newts leave the water at the end of the summer.

## From tadpole to frog

Early in the spring, frogs lay their eggs, which are called frogspawn, in ponds. The tiny tadpoles that hatch do not look like frogs at first, but they change as they grow. If you keep going back to a pond where you find frogspawn, you can watch what happens.

Frogs have smooth, moist skin.

Gills for breathing

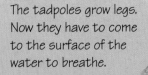

Frogs lay their eggs in clumps of clear jelly which float to the surface of a pond.

After about ten days, tadpoles wiggle out. They swim in search of food and soon grow.

The tadpoles grow legs. Now they have to come to the surface of the water to breathe.

After 12 or 13 weeks, the tadpoles have turned into tiny frogs, ready to leave the water.

# Decorated eggs

Get out your poster paints, cut out some flower pictures and you can create your own collection of decorated eggs. Here you can find out how to make speckled eggs, flowery eggs and sparkling eggs. Before you decorate the eggs, you will need to blow them to empty them out. Ask an adult to help you do this. Always hold eggs very carefully, as they can break easily.

## You will need

Eggs
A large needle
A small bowl
An eggbox
Poster paints
Water
Clear glue with a fine nozzle

Paintbrushes
Scissors
Clear varnish
Flowered gift wrap or magazine pictures of flowers
Sequins
Ribbons

## Blowing the eggs

**1.** Make a hole in one end of each egg with the needle. Make a bigger hole at the other end.

**2.** Hold the egg over the bowl. Blow hard into the small hole so that all the egg comes out of the big hole.

**3.** Rinse the egg under cold water. Dry it carefully then stand it, big hole down, to drain.

On farms, chicks hatch from eggs in the spring.

## Speckled eggs

**1.** Hold an egg in one hand. Starting at one end, paint half of it with thick, pale poster paint.

**2.** Let the paint dry, then paint the other half the same color in the same way. Let the paint dry again.

**3.** Use a stiff brush to splatter the eggs first with white paint and then with brown paint.

**4.** When the eggs are dry, add larger dots of white and brown using a fine paintbrush.

## Flowery and sparkling eggs

 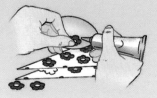  

**1.** Paint the eggs with thick white or gold poster paint, one half at a time, as above, then let the paint dry.

**2.** Cut out flowers and leaves from the gift wrap and glue them carefully to some of the eggs.

**3.** To make sparkling eggs, glue sequins to some of the eggs that you have painted gold.

**4.** When the glue has dried, paint the eggs with clear varnish. This helps to protect them.

Group your eggs attractively and display them in pretty baskets, clear glass jars or egg boxes painted in bright colors.

# Spring bunnies

These funny bunny faces taste like sausage rolls but look much nicer. Make them for a special spring treat. This recipe will make eight bunnies.

## You will need

2½ cups flour
12 tablespoons margarine
12 teaspoons cold water
½ cup sausage meat, browned
A pinch of salt
1 egg, beaten
A mixing bowl
A knife
A teaspoon
A rolling pin
A large round cookie cutter
A bottle top
A pastry brush
A fat straw
A spatula
A greased cookie sheet

Set the oven to 400°F

## What to do

**1.** Mix the flour and salt together. With your fingers, rub in the margarine until it looks like fine breadcrumbs.

**2.** Add the water. Use a knife to mix the water into the flour. Squeeze the mixture into a ball.

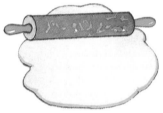

**3.** Sprinkle some flour on a work surface and the rolling pin. Roll the pastry ball out thinly and evenly.

**4.** For each rabbit cut out three big circles and two small ones. Roll up eight small balls of pastry.

Look for rabbits in the fields in spring.

**5.** Brush one of the big circles with beaten egg, then put a teaspoon of sausage meat in the middle.

**6.** Lay one of the other big circles on top. Press your finger all around the edges to join the circles together.

**7.** Brush the top circles with egg. Lift the pastry cases onto the baking tray with the spatula.

**8.** Press two of the small circles onto each pastry case for cheeks. Press on a small ball for a nose.

**9.** Use the cookie cutter to cut out an ear from each side of one of the remaining big circles.

**10.** Press the ears onto the top of the pastry faces. Brush the ears, noses and cheeks with beaten egg.

**11.** Use the end of the straw to make eyes for each bunny. Then bake them in the oven for about 15 minutes, until golden.

Rabbits are always on the lookout, with their ears twitching and noses quivering.

# Spot the babies

Spring is the season when many animals have their babies. The weather is warmer, there is plenty of food to eat and the young animals have time to grow big and strong before winter comes again. Most young animals leave their mothers soon after they are born and quickly learn how to find their own food and take care of themselves.

At first, lambs just drink their mothers' milk, but after 14 weeks they start to eat grass.

Ducklings and other baby birds have fluffy down to keep them warm before their feathers grow.

## Lambs

Sheep have their lambs early in the spring. Most mother sheep have one to three babies. A mother can recognize her own lambs bleating among hundreds of others in a field.

## Ducklings

Look for ducklings bobbing along behind their mothers in ponds, rivers and lakes. Mother ducks take their new ducklings to the water's edge. The ducklings fall in and can swim right away. When there is danger nearby, the mother duck quacks loudly and the ducklings dive underwater.

## Baby birds

Birds build their nests and lay their eggs in spring. Look for birds carrying grass, twigs or pieces of fluff. This is usually a sign that they are building a nest. Once they have laid their eggs and the chicks have hatched, you may see the parent birds flying to and from the nest carrying worms or other food.

Never disturb breeding birds or their nests and eggs. It is against the law. Always watch from a distance.

A song thrush arriving back at its nest with food

## Piglets

Pigs have several babies at a time. The piglets push and shove to drink their mother's milk. Newborn piglets have to take care of themselves. Their mother does not clean them or help them to feed. They start eating solid food when they are three weeks old.

Piglets are curious and playful.

## Fox cubs

Fox cubs are born underground in a big burrow called an earth. For the first month they stay with their mother in their earth, feeding on her milk. After that, she brings food back to the earth. By summer the cubs have started hunting on their own.

Fox cubs start to leave the earth to play when they are a few weeks old.

# Caterpillar tracks

Spring is a good time to look for caterpillars. You might spot some in a garden or out in the country. Many of them live on leaves but you may also find one wiggling across a path in search of its food plant.

## Caterpillar to pupa

A caterpillar hatches from an egg laid by a butterfly or moth.

The tiny caterpillar eats and eats and grows bigger and bigger.

Then it makes a hard case called a pupa around itself.

A caterpillar has five pairs of fleshy back legs called claspers for clinging onto things.

## Inside the pupa

Inside a pupa, the caterpillar turns into a butterfly (or moth). After a few weeks, the pupa skin splits and the butterfly breaks out. It stretches its wings and flies away.

Butterfly on a buddleia flower

## Where to find caterpillars

Caterpillars eat leaves. Look for them both on the top and underside of leaves and grasses. Most caterpillars eat just one kind of leaf. Many of them are green, which makes them hard to spot against the leaves, but if you search carefully you may spot one.

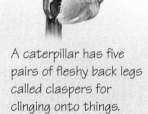

Some caterpillars spin a tent out of silky thread and eat the leaves inside it.

The caterpillars of some tiny moths tunnel inside a leaf to eat it. Some caterpillars eat around themselves. Others move forward as they eat.

# Summer

# The night sky in summer

The sky never gets really dark in summer, so only the brightest stars can be seen clearly. The best time to use these maps is at around 11pm on a clear night, away from city lights.

## Maps for northern half of world

The maps on this page show the stars that people in the northern half of the world can see in summer, looking north and looking south. Looking north, the bright yellow star known as Capella hangs just above the horizon, with Regulus off to its left and the bright star Deneb high up in the east.

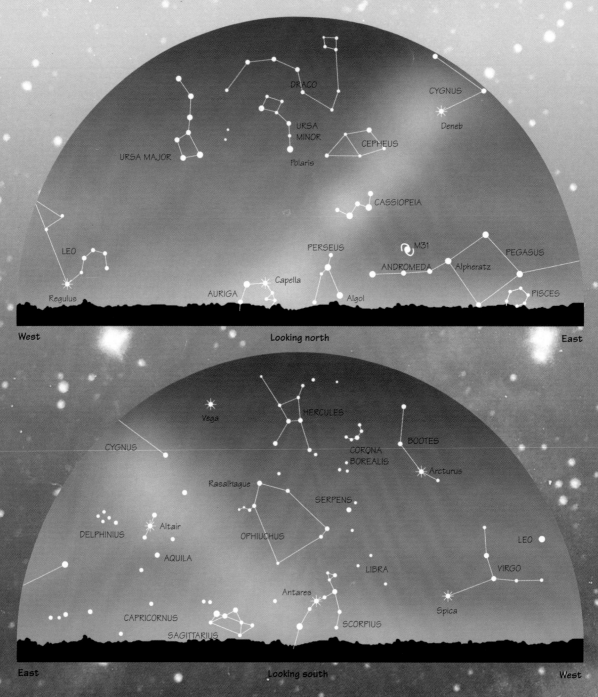

DRACO

CYGNUS

Deneb

URSA
MINOR

CEPHEUS

URSA MAJOR

Polaris

CASSIOPEIA

LEO

PERSEUS

M31

PEGASUS

ANDROMEDA    Alpheratz

Regulus

AURIGA    Capella

Algol

PISCES

**West**    **Looking north**    **East**

Vega

HERCULES

CYGNUS

CORONA
BOREALIS

BOOTES

Rasalhague

Arcturus

SERPENS

DELPHINIUS    Altair

OPHIUCHUS

LEO

AQUILA

VIRGO

LIBRA

Antares

Spica

CAPRICORNUS

SCORPIUS

SAGITTARIUS

**East**    **Looking south**    **West**

# Maps for southern half of world

These maps show the stars that people in the southern half of the world can see in summer. Facing north, the easiest constellations to spot are Orion and Canis Major (the Great Dog) and over to the east you can see Leo (the Lion).

Sirius (the Dog Star), one of the stars in Canis Major, is the brightest star in the sky. Orion was a great hunter in Greek mythology and the famous constellation named after him contains many bright stars. Look for the three stars that form Orion's belt.

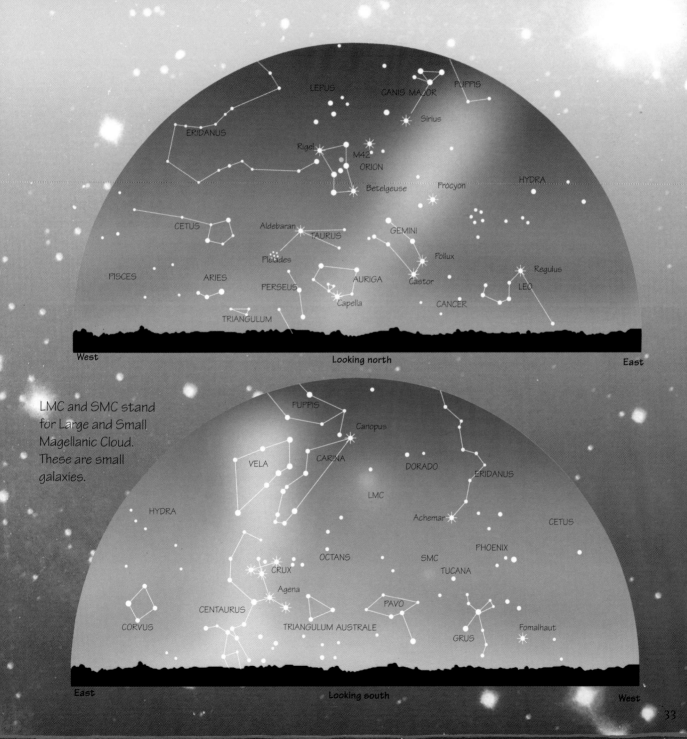

LEPUS   CANIS MAJOR   PUPPIS

Sirius

ERIDANUS

Rigel   M42   ORION

Betelgeuse   Procyon   HYDRA

CETUS   Aldebaran   TAURUS   GEMINI

Pleiades   Pollux

PISCES   ARIES   AURIGA   Castor   Regulus

PERSEUS   CANCER   LEO

Capella

TRIANGULUM

**West**     **Looking north**     **East**

LMC and SMC stand for Large and Small Magellanic Cloud. These are small galaxies.

PUPPIS

Canopus

VELA   CARINA   DORADO   ERIDANUS

LMC

HYDRA   Achernar   CETUS

PHOENIX

OCTANS   SMC   TUCANA

CRUX   Agena

Agena   PAVO

CENTAURUS   TRIANGULUM AUSTRALE   Fomalhaut

CORVUS   GRUS

**East**     **Looking south**     **West**

# What's the time?

In summer, the days are longer and the nights shorter than at any other time of the year. Midsummer's day is the longest day of the year. The sun also rises higher in the sky than it does during the other seasons. Check to see where it rises and sets each day.

## Shadow clock

You can find out how the sun changes position during the day by making a shadow clock with a friend. You will need to do this on a sunny day in a place where you are allowed to draw on the ground with chalk.

**1.** In the morning, ask your friend to stand with their feet together. Draw around their shoes and shadow with chalk. Then write down the time above the shadow.

**2.** Every two hours, do the same thing in the same spot. Write down the time above each shadow outline. Look how the position and shape of the shadow have changed during the day.

## What happens

As the sun rises high in the sky in the middle of the day, shadows become shorter. As the sun moves across the sky during the day, shadows change the direction they point in because they always point away from the sun.

*Shadows are longer in the morning and evening when the sun is low in the sky.*

# Sundials

Sundials have been used to tell the time for thousands of years. You can still see them in some places. A sundial is a very simple type of clock that uses a shadow to tell the time. Try making a sundial of your own. You will need to keep it in the same place once you have made it.

The upright part of a sundial is called a gnomon. Its shadow falls onto a flat dial marked similarly to a clock face.

What time was this picture taken?

## Make a sundial

### You will need
A flowerpot
A ruler
A black marker
Modeling clay
A stick twice the height of the flowerpot

**1.** Turn the flowerpot upside down. Push the stick through the hole in the pot and into the ground.

**2.** Wedge modeling clay around the stick, as shown, to hold it upright and keep it in place.

**3.** Mark where the stick's shadow is by drawing a line on the pot. Write the time next to the line.

**4.** Do the same thing again every hour. Now you will be able to tell the time on sunny days.

# Tomato feast

Home grown vegetables taste delicious and you don't even need a garden. Here you can find out how to grow tomatoes in pots. Plant them at the beginning of summer and you should have tomatoes by the end of the season.

## You will need

| | |
|---|---|
| Some small tomato plants | Small stones or gravel |
| Large pots | Canes |
| Special tomato compost | Garden ties |
| | A trowel |
| | A watering can |

## What to do

**1.** For each plant, put small stones in the bottom of a pot. This will stop the compost from getting soggy.

**2.** Cover the stones with compost so the pot is about a third full. Gently tip each plant out of its pot.

**3.** Carefully stand a tomato plant on top of the compost in each pot. Try not to squash the leaves.

*Tomatoes start off green and turn red when they are ripe.*

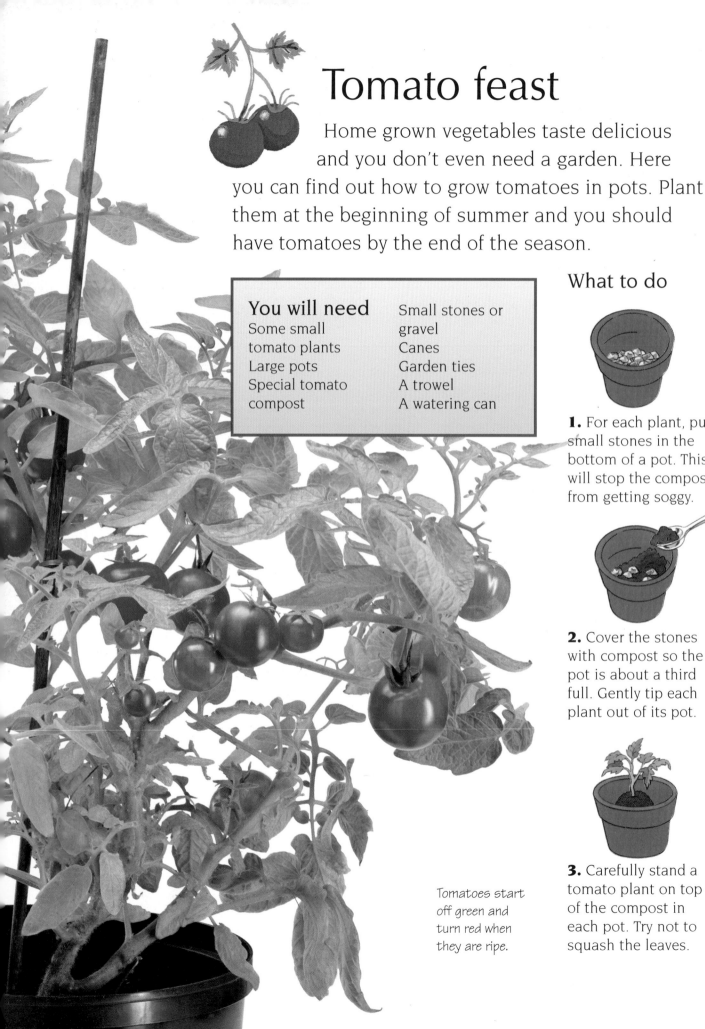

**4.** Fill in around each plant with more compost. Press the compost carefully so the plant stands firm.

**5.** Water the compost, then put the plants outside in a warm, sunny, sheltered place.

**6.** Water the plants a little every day to keep the compost damp, especially if the weather is hot.

**7.** As the plants grow taller and flower, carefully push a cane into each pot and tie the stem to it.

*You can make a delicious salad from sliced tomatoes and mozzarella cheese, garnished with fresh basil leaves.*

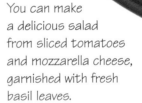

## Picking tomatoes

With plenty of warmth and water, the tomatoes will swell and turn red. This means that they are ripe and ready to pick. Pick them with the stalk still on the tomato and store them in the refrigerator if you are not going to eat them right away.

**8.** If you are lucky, each flower will form a tomato. A small bunch of tomatoes is called a truss.

**9.** When a plant has three trusses, pinch off the top of the main stem to stop it from growing taller.

*To make stuffed tomatoes, scoop out the middle of some big tomatoes and stuff them with cooked rice, peas, diced pepper and corn.*

# Strawberry trifle

This strawberry trifle is a lovely dessert to make for a special occasion on a hot summer's day. Try to make sure that you use the ripest, sweetest strawberries you can find and make sure you allow yourself plenty of time to prepare the trifle. Remember that you need about three hours for the sponge cakes to go soft and you need to allow time for the trifle to chill in the refrigerator for a few hours before you serve it.

## You will need

1lb fresh strawberries
6 sponge cakes
2 tablespoons strawberry jelly
4 tablespoons apple juice
1 small lemon
1/2 pint whipping cream
Half a teaspoon
vanilla extract
2 tablespoons granulated
sugar

Serves four

# What to do

**1.** Rinse the strawberries under cold water, then cut around the stalks and cores with a small knife and pull them out.

**2.** Cut most of the strawberries in half, but leave a few whole ones. Put the halved strawberries in a big glass or china bowl.

**3.** Cut the sponge cakes in half. Spread each half with jelly then press them together again. Cut the sponge cakes into quarters.

**4.** Put the pieces of cake on top of the strawberries and mix them together. Sprinkle the apple juice over the top of them.

**5.** Cover the bowl with plastic wrap. Put it in the refrigerator for about three hours, until the pieces of sponge cake are soft.

**6.** Grate the yellow skin (the zest) from the lemon, using the small holes of a cheese grater. Scrape the zest off with a knife.

**7.** When the sponge mixture has chilled, pour the cream into a large bowl. Add the lemon zest, vanilla and sugar.

**8.** Beat the mixture with a whisk for several minutes until it becomes thicker and forms floppy peaks. It shouldn't be too stiff.

**9.** Spoon the whipping cream over the sponge mixture and spread it out. Refrigerate the trifle until you are ready to serve it.

39

# Summer flowers

By pressing flowers you can keep them for a long time and use them on pictures and cards. The easiest to press are open-faced flowers, such as pansies, or bell-shaped ones. Press flowers as soon as you pick them, so they do not wilt, and always ask permission first.

## Pressing flowers

### You will need
Common or garden flowers, such as pansies, larkspur and violets
Heavy books
Tissue paper

**1.** Pick fresh, undamaged flowers that have fully opened. They should be dry, not wet with rain or dew.

**2.** Put paper on one side of an open book. Lay flowers on it so they are flat and not touching.

*Pressed fuchsia flowers*

**3.** Lay another piece of paper on top of the flowers. Smooth it down carefully, then close the book.

**4.** Stack more books on top. Leave the flowers in the book for four weeks, to dry and flatten out.

## Making pictures

### You will need
Thick paper or thin cardboard
Scissors and glue
Cotton balls
Clear plastic film

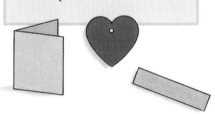

**1.** Cut out pieces of thick paper or cardboard for the bases of your pictures, gift tags or bookmarks.

**2.** Lay pressed flowers and leaves on each piece of cardboard and paper. Try out different arrangements.

**3.** Dab a tiny dot of glue on the back of each flower and leaf, then stick them down in position.

**4.** Cut pieces of plastic film bigger than the cardboard. Cover the cardboard with the film and trim the edges

## Seasonal flowers

Summer is a good time to press flowers because there is a wide variety to choose from, but of course you can also press them in the spring and even the fall. Be very careful when you handle any pressed plants, as they are very delicate and break easily.

## Flower picture

Arrange pressed flowers, leaves and ferns on a piece of thick, textured paper. You could arrange them to look as if they are growing naturally, or make a pattern with them.

## Bookmark

Use a narrow strip of thin cardboard to make a bookmark. This shape works best with small delicate flowers and leaves.

## Gift tags

To make gift tags, glue the pressed flowers and leaves onto small pieces of thin cardboard. Punch a hole in each tag and thread a ribbon through it to attach it to the gift.

*A picture, bookmark and gift tag, all decorated with pressed flowers, leaves and ferns*

# Bugwatch

In summer, you only have to turn over a stone, dig up some soil or look at any plant to come across countless insects and other tiny creatures. They are all around you in gardens, fields, woods, ponds, streams and on the seashore. Watch what they do and you can learn a lot about how animals live.

A bumblebee gathering nectar and pollen from a flower

## Bees

Bees feed on nectar, a sweet liquid found inside most flowers. Most bees gather nectar from one type of flower at a time. As a bee flies from flower to flower, it also gathers pollen, the sticky yellow dust inside flowers. It carries the pollen to other flowers and this helps the flowers to make new seeds.

## Dragonflies

Look for dragonflies flying low above ponds and streams early in the summer. Their brightly colored bodies flash as they swoop across the water, chasing insects. You may see them rest on leaves, their wings outstretched in the sun.

Peacock butterfly

## Butterflies

Butterflies and moths are attracted to brightly colored, scented flowers. Like bees, they feed on nectar. Watch how they stretch out a long, thin tube called a proboscis as soon as they land on a flower. They use this proboscis like a drinking straw to suck up the sweet nectar.

Close-up of a butterfly's head and proboscis

Dragonflies have four gauzy wings.

## Ants

Ants live together in enormous groups called colonies. They make nests by burrowing in sand or soil. If you watch where a line of ants goes, you will probably find their nest hole. The ants work hard, carrying food and other things back to their colony. They leave a scent trail between the food they find and the nest, so that the rest of the ants know which way to go.

Wood ants carrying food back to their nest

Dung beetles gather animal dung and roll it into a ball. They eat some of it and lay eggs in the rest.

## Beetles

Beetles have hardened front wings that protect their delicate flying wings. Look for them under bark and stones or around trash heaps. They eat all kinds of plants and animals. There are thousands of different beetles living everywhere. See how many you can find.

Beetles are the most heavily armored of all the insects.

Devil's coach horse beetle

Green shield bug

## In the soil

If you dig around in the soil, you may find grubs or larvae. These are baby insects. Many insects, such as beetles and flies, lay their eggs in the soil. When the larvae hatch, they stay under the ground and eat the roots of plants. Some larvae stay under the ground for several years before they change into insects and go up above the ground.

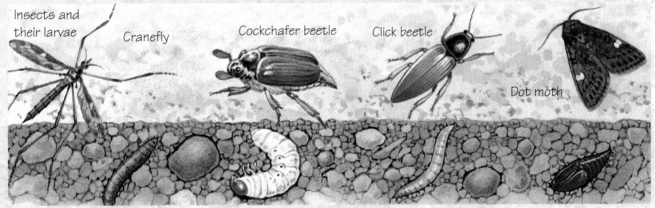

Insects and their larvae

Cranefly

Cockchafer beetle

Click beetle

Dot moth

# Snail trail

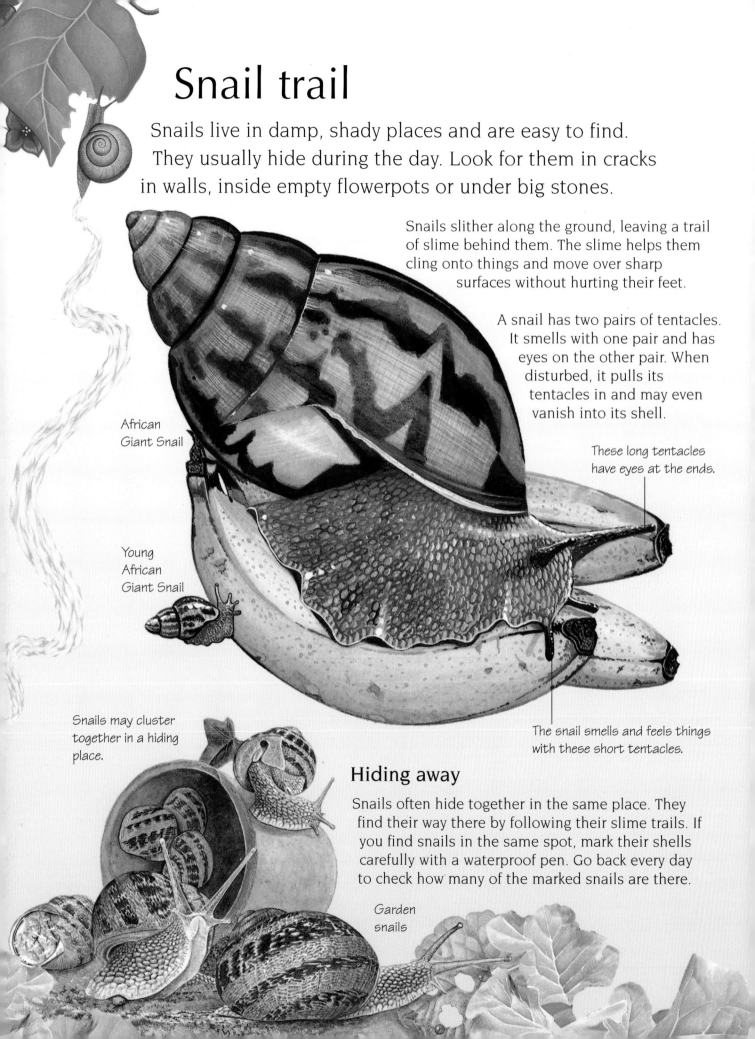

Snails live in damp, shady places and are easy to find. They usually hide during the day. Look for them in cracks in walls, inside empty flowerpots or under big stones.

Snails slither along the ground, leaving a trail of slime behind them. The slime helps them cling onto things and move over sharp surfaces without hurting their feet.

A snail has two pairs of tentacles. It smells with one pair and has eyes on the other pair. When disturbed, it pulls its tentacles in and may even vanish into its shell.

African Giant Snail

These long tentacles have eyes at the ends.

Young African Giant Snail

Snails may cluster together in a hiding place.

The snail smells and feels things with these short tentacles.

## Hiding away

Snails often hide together in the same place. They find their way there by following their slime trails. If you find snails in the same spot, mark their shells carefully with a waterproof pen. Go back every day to check how many of the marked snails are there.

Garden snails

## Snail shells

Shells protect snails' soft bodies. Baby snails have soft shells which harden as they grow. If you look at a snail's shell, you can see lines. The distance between them shows how much the snail has grown in a year.

## Snail enemy

Some birds, such as thrushes, eat snails. They pick up a snail in their beak and smash the shell against a stone so they can eat the snail inside. Pieces of shell are left around the stone.

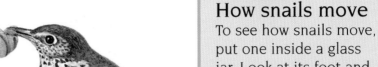

A thrush breaks a snail's shell by smashing it on a stone.

## How snails move

To see how snails move, put one inside a glass jar. Look at its foot and you will see ripples pushing it forward.

## Snail eggs

In the summer you sometimes find snails slithering over each other. This means they are mating. Afterward, each snail lays its eggs in a hole in the soil. Look for clusters of round, white eggs buried just beneath the soil.

A snail and its eggs

## Feeding habits

Snails usually come out to feed at night, or after rain. This is because their skin isn't waterproof and they die if they dry out. In winter, or in hot weather, snails hide in shady spots. They close themselves into their shells with slime which sets into a hard seal. Most snails feed on plants and are especially fond of soft growing shoots.

Snails eat by filing off bits of leaves with rows of tiny teeth on their tongues.

Snails feed on soft growing shoots.

# Beachcombing

If you go to a beach, you can have fun looking for shells, pebbles and other treasures. It is best to explore at low tide when the sea is out. Try looking along the line of seaweed that marks the high water level at the top of the beach.

Spider conch
Cat's paw scallop
Prickly cockle
Wentletraps
Cone shells
Top shells
Oysters
Violet sea snails
Tiger cowrie
Moon shells
Serpent's head cowries
Jingle shells
Calico clam
Venus clams
Coquina clams
Beautiful tellin
Limpets
Razor shells
Watermelon tellins
Queen scallops
Mussels
Common whelks
Abalones

## Collecting shells

You will find shells on most beaches. They were made by tiny animals which lived inside them. When the animals died, their shells were left behind and washed ashore. Only collect empty shells. If you pick up a shell with an animal in it, put it back where you found it.

Shells come in many shapes and sizes. Gastropods are single shells and are often coiled. Bivalves come in pairs, joined by a little hinge. See if you can find any of the shells shown here.

## How to collect

**1.** Use buckets or plastic bags for collecting shells. Label the bags to say where you found the shells.

**2.** When you get home, soak the shells in warm, soapy water. Gently scrub them clean with an old toothbrush.

**3.** Some shells come in pairs. Wrap some thread around them to keep them together while they dry.

**4.** Store fragile shells on cotton batting in a box. Display the others on a tray or a box lid.

## Pebbles and other finds

Look for interesting stones along rocky beaches. Pebbles come in many colors and sizes, depending on the rock they are made of. You may find pieces of colored glass that have been worn smooth by the sea. On some beaches you may find interesting pieces of driftwood, or even some fossils.

This fossil ammonite shows the shape of the animal's shell.

Fossils in limestone

Sea glass

## Fossils

Fossils are the remains of animals that lived long ago. Very slowly, as the years went by, their remains turned to stone.

Driftwood

Calcite vein

Seaweed

Flints

## Starfish

You might find a starfish washed up on a rocky beach. Starfish usually have five arms which are covered in small bumps and have suckers underneath.

Common starfish (below) are orange. Spiny starfish (right) are purple or brown.

Pebble made of marble fragments

Quartz veins

# Beach treasures

There are lots of things you can do with the treasures you have collected from the beach. You could make a display tray to show them off, create attractive paperweights or decorate boxes and picture frames.

## Display tray

### You will need

A large pizza box
Newspaper
A craft knife
Thin white cardboard

Used matchsticks
Felt or colored paper
A pen
Tape

**1.** Fill the pizza box with crumpled newspaper. Tape the lid shut. Tape around the corners of the box as well.

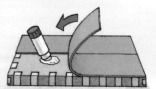

**2.** Glue colored paper or felt to the top and sides of the box. Cut several pieces and join them neatly.

**3.** Arrange your collection on the box. Mark several dots around the edge of each object with a pen.

**4.** Remove the objects from the box. Carefully cut a tiny cross over each dot, as shown, with the craft knife.

*Use the display tray as a showcase for your collections of fossils, pebbles or seashells.*

**5.** Push a matchstick into each hole, with the used end down. Leave about 1cm (½in) of each matchstick showing.

**6.** Put the objects back, so the matchsticks hold them in place. Make a card label for each object.

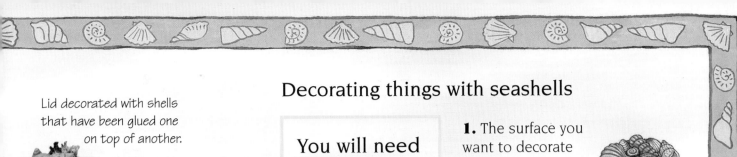

Lid decorated with shells that have been glued one on top of another.

Shells glued to a picture frame

# Decorating things with seashells

## You will need

Different-shaped seashells
Box lids, picture frames or hair clips
PVA glue
Clear varnish
A paintbrush

**1.** The surface you want to decorate must be clean and dry. Arrange some shells on top of it.

**2.** Glue on the shells. Pick up one shell at a time, dab glue on it, and press it in place.

**3.** When the glue has dried, paint the shells with varnish. Let it dry, then paint a second coat.

Keep unpainted pebbles in water to make them look bright.

Funny face pebbles

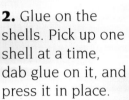

Use small shells to decorate a plain hairclip or headband.

## Painted pebbles

## You will need

Large, smooth pebbles
Poster or acrylic paints
A thick paintbrush
A thin paintbrush
Clear varnish

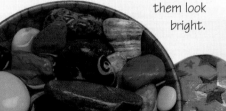

Cat paperweight

Patterned paperweights

**1.** Wash each pebble and let it dry. Paint it all over with a thick coat of white paint and let it dry.

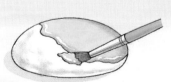

**2.** Paint the pebble with whichever color you want to use as your base. Let the paint dry again.

**3.** Paint a picture. Do the outlines first and let them dry. Then add details with a fine brush.

**4.** When the paint has dried, paint a coat of varnish over it and let it dry. This protects the paint.

# Harvest time

Many different foods and drinks are made from plants. Fruit and vegetables come from plants, but so do other everyday foods, such as flour, coffee, cocoa, cooking oil and sugar. Most plant foods are grown as crops and are picked or harvested in the summer.

Sunflower seeds are in the middle of the flowers.

## Grain crops

Look for combine harvesters working in fields late in the summer. These huge machines harvest crops such as wheat, oats, rye and barley that are grown for their seeds or grain. Combine harvesters don't just cut the crop, they also gather it together and separate the grain from the stalks. The grain is ground into flour or used to make breakfast cereals.

## Sunflowers

In some countries with warm climates, sunflowers are grown as a crop. The sunflower seeds are harvested and used to make cooking oil.

Cherries

Strawberries and raspberries

## Corn

Corn is a tall leafy plant grown for its plump yellow cobs of grain. Most corn is grown for animal feed, but it is also used to make cooking oil, breakfast cereals and popcorn. Some sweet varieties are sold as corn on the cob.

Corn on the cob

## Soft fruits

Soft fruits are ripe and ready to pick in the summer. They are sometimes grown on farms where people can go and pick the fruit themselves.

Gooseberries

Blackcurrants

# Fall

# The night sky in fall

These star maps will help you identify the constellations that you can see in the night sky in fall. The best time to use the maps is at around 11pm on a clear night, away from city lights.

## Maps for northern half of world

Facing north, look out for Ursa Major which is below the Pole Star and parallel with the horizon. Looking south, you should be able to see Pegasus (the Winged Horse), which has a square of stars in the middle. The single star Fomalhaut flashes just above the horizon, and to the east Altair shines brightly.

This is the best time to see M31, a huge, distant galaxy . It is just visible with the naked eye.

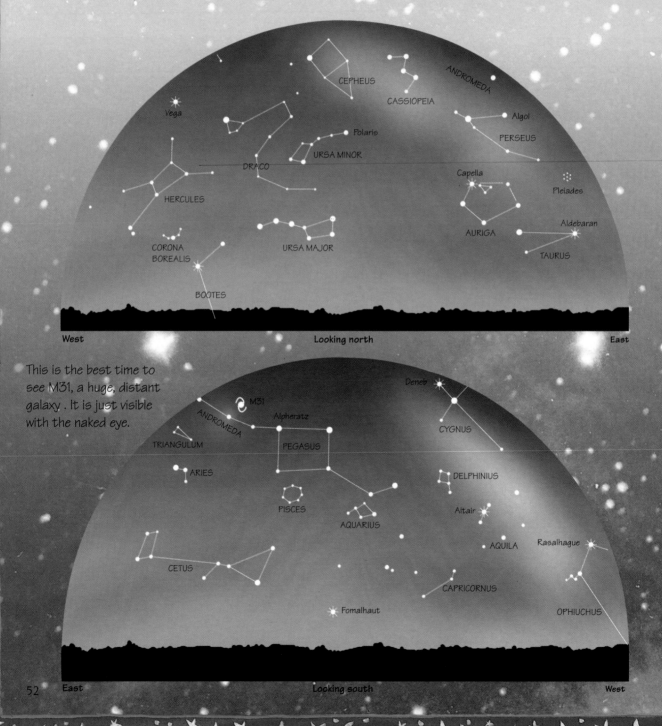

CEPHEUS

ANDROMEDA

CASSIOPEIA

Vega

Algol

PERSEUS

Polaris

URSA MINOR

DRACO

Capella

Pleiades

HERCULES

Aldebaran

CORONA BOREALIS

URSA MAJOR

AURIGA

TAURUS

BOOTES

West        Looking north        East

Deneb

M31

ANDROMEDA        Alpheratz

CYGNUS

TRIANGULUM        PEGASUS

ARIES        DELPHINIUS

Altair

PISCES

AQUARIUS        AQUILA        Rasalhague

CETUS

CAPRICORNUS        OPHIUCHUS

Fomalhaut

East        Looking south        West

# Maps for southern half of world

Looking north, a triangle of three bright stars dominates the sky: Regulus, which is blue, yellow Arcturus and blue-white Spica. Also look for the constellations of Virgo (the Virgin) and Leo (the Lion).

Looking south, the Milky Way crosses the sky in a wide band. Crux (the southern Cross) is almost overhead. Above it is Centaurus (the Centaur). A centaur in Greek mythology is a creature that is half man and half horse.

LMC and SMC stand for Large and Small Magellanic Cloud. These are small galaxies.

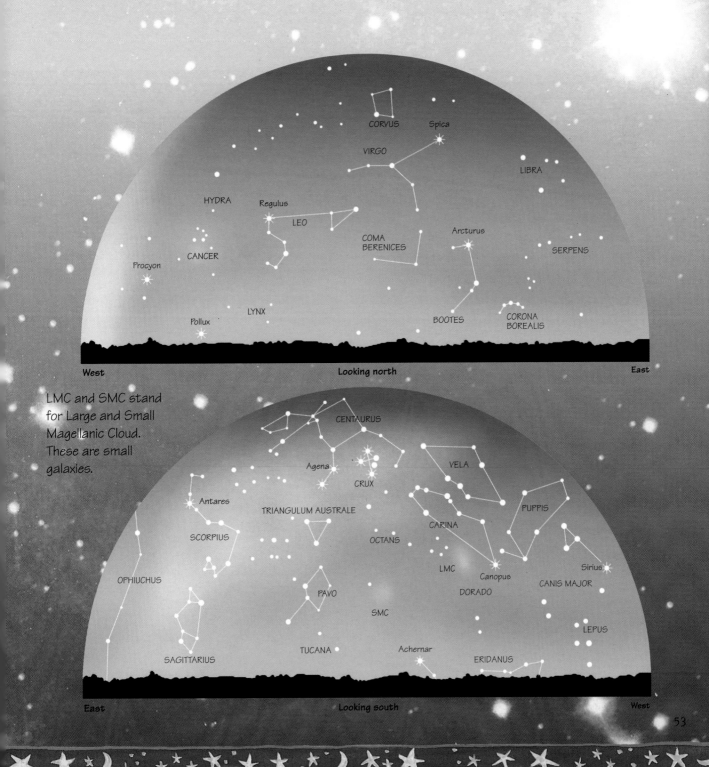

CORVUS
Spica
VIRGO
LIBRA
HYDRA
Regulus
LEO
COMA BERENICES
Arcturus
SERPENS
CANCER
Procyon
LYNX
Pollux
BOOTES
CORONA BOREALIS

**West**      Looking north      **East**

CENTAURUS
Agena
VELA
CRUX
Antares
TRIANGULUM AUSTRALE
PUPPIS
SCORPIUS
CARINA
OCTANS
LMC
Sirius
Canopus
OPHIUCHUS
PAVO
DORADO
CANIS MAJOR
SMC
LEPUS
SAGITTARIUS
TUCANA
Achernar
ERIDANUS

**East**      Looking south      **West**

# Everlasting flowers

In the fall, you can use dried flowers and leaves to decorate your home. Look for interesting plants that are drying out naturally, seed heads, bracken, reeds and grasses.

## You will need

A strong rubber band for each type of flower
String
Scissors

## Drying flowers

Good flowers to dry are statice, sea thistles, strawflowers, lavender, love-in-a-mist and poppy seed heads. Choose flowers that are almost fully open, and pick them with long stems. Always ask an adult before you pick anything.

**1.** Pick the flowers on a dry day, once any dew has dried. Sort each type of flower into a separate bunch.

**2.** Strip the lower leaves off the stems. Fasten each bunch of flowers together tightly with a rubber band.

**3.** Fan the flower heads out a little so that they aren't touching each other. This keeps them from rotting.

**4.** Hang the bunches upside down in a cool, airy place away from direct sunlight, such as a garage or shed.

Leave the flowers until they have dried out completely. Handle them carefully when you take them down as they will be quite delicate and may snap easily.

Dried flowers look good packed into baskets or jugs, so that you can see the flowers but not the stems. Try different arrangements to see what looks best.

Lavender, statice, strawflowers and dried poppy seed heads

# Preserving leaves

You can preserve fall leaves with glycerin (from a pharmacy). They will darken a little, but still look fresh and natural. Choose large sprays of tree leaves in different colors.

**1.** Mix together ½ pint glycerin with 1½ pints hot water in a pitcher or large jar.

**2.** Ask an adult to help you cut a slit about 2in long at the end of each stem of leaves.

**3.** Put the branches in the pitcher. If they drink a lot of the mixture, make more and fill it up.

**4.** When the leaves begin to darken, take them out of the pitcher and tie them together with string.

**5.** Hang the leaves upside down in a dark, dry place. Leave them until they have dried out completely.

*Arrange the dried leaves in a big pitcher or vase to create a dramatic effect.*

# Fruits and seeds

In late summer and fall, trees produce seeds. Some come in nuts, others are encased in juicy fruits or tucked away in cones. In fact, all these things are fruits and do the same job. They protect the seeds inside and help them spread to a new place where they can grow. See how many of these different kinds of tree seeds you can find.

Seeds

Rowan

Fruit

## The seeds of broadleaved trees

Broadleaved trees all produce seeds inside fruits. These may be hard nuts, berries or soft fruits.

Nuts have hard outer shells. These have to break or rot before the seeds inside them can start to grow into new trees.

These fruits contain seeds.

Sweet chestnut

Fruit

Edible seed

Fruit

Seeds

Fig

Ash fruits have wings. These spin in the wind to carry the seeds away.

Soft fruits and berries are eaten by birds and animals. They drop the seeds inside the fruits, spreading them to new places.

## Conifer seeds

Conifers are trees that produce their seeds in cones. Most cones have woody scales that open in warm, dry weather to release the seeds. The scales close when it is wet.

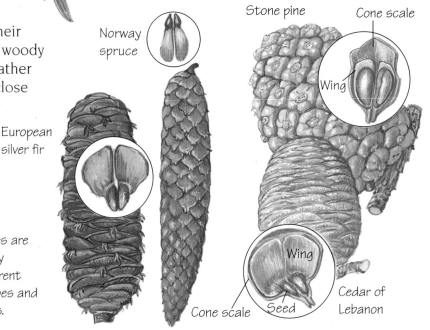

Norway spruce

Stone pine

Cone scale

Wing

European silver fir

Larch cones sometimes stay on a tree for many years.

Cones are many different shapes and sizes.

European larch

Wing

Cone scale    Seed

Cedar of Lebanon

56

# Seed bracelet and necklace

Look for interesting large tree seeds and flower seed heads that you can collect to make into a necklace or bracelet.

## Bracelet

**1.** Choose the seeds you want and lay them out in the order or pattern you want to use them.

**2.** Cut a piece of thin elastic long enough to go around your wrist. Thread the elastic onto the needle.

**3.** Carefully pierce each seed one at a time with the needle, then thread it onto the elastic. Tie the ends together.

## Necklace

**1.** Thread the seeds onto a length of strong thread long enough to make a necklace.

**2.** When all the seeds are threaded, tie the ends of the thread together in a knot.

This necklace is made of small fir cones sprayed gold, poppy seed heads, senna pods, sunflower seeds and pumpkin seeds.

# Fruity crumble

You can use most kinds of fruit for this wonderful dessert with a crunchy crumble topping. It is very good made with apples, but you could also make it with half apples and half blackberries, or use other fall fruits, such as plums or pears.

## What to do

**1.** Peel the apples, cut them into quarters and cut out the cores. Slice them and put them in the dish.

**2.** Add the apple juice or water, the cinnamon and sugar and stir everything together well.

  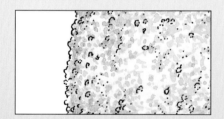

**3.** Sift both types of flour into a mixing bowl. Cut the butter into small cubes and add it to the bowl.

**4.** Rub the butter into the flour with your fingertips, lifting the mixture and letting it fall back into the bowl.

**5.** When the mixture looks like coarse breadcrumbs, add the brown sugar. Mix this in with your hands too.

## You will need

1½ lbs. eating apples
3 tablespoons apple juice or water
½ teaspoon ground cinnamon
1 tablespoon sugar
1 cup all-purpose flour
1 cup wheat flour
¾ cup butter
¾ cup light soft brown sugar
A medium casserole dish

Set the oven to: 400°F

Serves six

*Plums, apples and blackberries all make excellent crumbles.*

Try making crumble with different types of apples, to see which you like best.

**6.** Spread this crumble mixture over the apple and press it down firmly with a fork. Put the dish on a baking sheet.

**7.** Put the crumble on the middle shelf of the oven and bake it for 35 to 40 minutes, until the topping is golden brown.

**8.** Push the tip of a knife into a piece of the apple. If it's not soft, put the crumble back into the oven for five more minutes.

## Serving the crumble

When the crumble has cooked and the apple is soft, take it out of the oven and leave it to cool for 10 to 15 minutes before you serve it. Fruit crumbles are delicious served warm with whipped cream or a dollop of vanilla ice cream. Any leftover crumble tastes good reheated or eaten cold the following day.

Warm fruity crumble with vanilla ice cream

# Fall leaves

In the fall, the leaves of many trees drop to the ground. Trees that lose their leaves like this are called deciduous trees. Most of them have soft, flat leaves. These often change color before they fall, and turn red, yellow, orange or brown. Here you can find out how to press fall leaves to keep in a scrapbook and how to make leaf prints.

English oak (rounded lobes)

Field maple (jagged)

Common lime (heart-shaped)

## Leaf shapes

Leaves are many different shapes and sizes. Some are a simple shape. Others are split into several parts, have zigzag edges or rounded lobes. All trees breathe and feed with their leaves. The green color in the leaves makes food from air and water while the leaves are in daylight.

## Leaves close-up

The upper surface of a leaf is tough and often glossy to stop the sun from drying it out. If you look closely at the underside of a green leaf, you will see a network of tiny veins running through it.

Fall leaves. From the left, clockwise: Red oak, Copper beech, Ginkgo, Rowan, Common pear.

Close-up, showing the veins on the underside of a leaf

## Changing color

In the fall, it is not warm enough for soft leaves to make much food. A corky layer grows across the leaf stalk, cutting off the water supply to the leaf. The leaf changes color, dries out and dies.

# Make a leaf scrapbook

## You will need
Fall leaves
Sheets of tissue paper
A heavy book
A heavy object

**1.** Lay the leaves between sheets of tissue paper, so they don't touch. Put the book and weight on top.

**2.** After a few weeks the leaves will be flat and dry. Tape them into a scrapbook and label them.

*If you find skeletons of old leaves, put them in a scrapbook too.*

# Leaf prints

## You will need
Different shaped leaves
Poster paints
Thick paper
Scrap paper

**1.** Paint an even layer of paint over the underside of a leaf. Start at the middle and paint outward.

**2.** Gently lay the leaf paint-side down on the paper. Put scrap paper over the top and press it firmly all over.

**3.** Lift off the scrap paper, then carefully peel off the leaf. Use the tip of a knife to do this if it is difficult.

**4.** To make more delicate prints, print the leaf again three or four times without adding any more paint.

**5.** Make prints of different leaves in red, orange and yellow to create a striking fall leaf picture.

61

# Fall trees

As the trees change color in the fall, try drawing a picture of them with chalk pastels. These are good for drawing landscapes because they are soft and blend together very easily. Chalk pastels work really well on colored paper. For the best results, use thick paper with a textured surface.

## You will need
Colored Bristol paper or textured paper
Chalk pastels

## Mixing colors

You can mix pastels straight on your paper by drawing strokes of one color across strokes of another color.

*Experiment with different combinations of colors and shades.*

## Blocking

Use the side of a pastel to create blocks of color. Then go over them with blocks of different colors.

*Try different shapes, colors and patterns.*

## Hatching

Use the end of a pastel like a pencil to draw short diagonal lines. Then draw more short lines over them in different colors.

## Blending

To create a softer effect, try drawing overlapping strokes in different colors.

Then gently smudge them together with the tip of your finger, or you could use a cotton swab.

# Fall landscape

**1.** Block in the sky, with a turquoise chalk pastel. Leave a blank area of paper for the trees.

**2.** Add patches of pale blue to the sky. Then block in small patches of dark blue over the top.

**3.** Block in the shapes of different colored trees with yellow, orange and rust pastels.

**4.** Hatch over each tree with darker or contrasting colors. Let the colors blend together.

**5.** Block in stripes of green, yellow and orange to look like a field in the foreground.

**6.** Hatch across the stripes with orange and brown. Make the stripes longer in the foreground.

**7.** Use a black pastel to draw a line below the trees, then draw the tree trunks and branches.

# Toadstool hunt

Early fall is the best time to go hunting for toadstools and mushrooms. You can find an astonishing variety in fields and forests, and even in gardens. All toadstools and mushrooms are fungi. These are plants that don't have any leaves or flowers but send tiny threads down into other plants or animal dung and feed on them. Some fungi grow among dead leaves; others grow on tree trunks or dead logs. Here are some to look for.

## Warning
Some toadstools are edible, but others that look similar are deadly poisonous. Do not pick toadstools unless you are with an adult, and never taste or eat toadstools you find.

Fly agaric toadstools look pretty but are actually poisonous.

Fairy ring toadstools
Often grow on lawns in a ring. The ring grows larger every year as the toadstools' underground threads reach out into fresh soil for food.

Cep
Edible. Has a dark brown cap with pores underneath, instead of gills. Usually grows under conifers.

Fly agaric
Poisonous. Usually grows under birch or pine trees, often in sandy soil.

**Stinkhorn**
Has a nasty strong smell. Grows in woods and hedges.

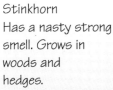

**Wood blewit**
Has a lilac tinge. Grows in woods.

**Birch bracket**
Has a creamish brown cap that splits with age, and white spores. Grows on birch trees, which it kills.

**Dryad's saddle**
Has a pale yellow-brown cap with darker scales. Grows on the trunks of broad-leaved trees.

**Honey fungus**
Has cream-colored gills that go brown with age. Grows at the base of trees, which it eventually kills.

**Crimson wax cap**
Grows in grass fields and along roadsides. Color of the cap fades with age.

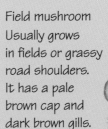

**Parasol**
Has white gills and a scaly cap. Grows in woods and grassy places.

**Field mushroom**
Usually grows in fields or grassy road shoulders. It has a pale brown cap and dark brown gills.

**Chanterelle**
Edible. Has fold-like ridges and smells of apricot. Grows in broad-leaved woods, especially beech and oak.

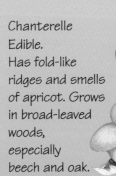

**Giant puffball**
One of the biggest fungi. Splits open when ripe. Grows in fields, woods and hedges.

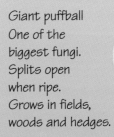
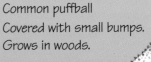

**Common puffball**
Covered with small bumps. Grows in woods.

# Silken webs

The best time to see spiders' webs is early on a fall morning, when their fragile threads are strung with beads of dew or mist. Spiders spin webs to catch insects. Different spiders build different types of webs. Here are some to look for.

Spiders use special organs in their abdomens to spin their silk threads.

## Orb webs

Garden spiders build orb webs. First, a spider spins a framework. Next, it spins spokes across the framework. It joins the spokes together with spirals of special sticky thread.

Spiders often build a new web every day, as webs are easily broken or damaged. You may find an old web with holes in it, or areas that a spider has repaired.

The spider lies in wait on its web, or hides under leaves, joined to the web by a thread. When an insect flies into the web, the web shakes and the spider rushes out to attack.

Spiders move across their webs very fast when the web shakes.

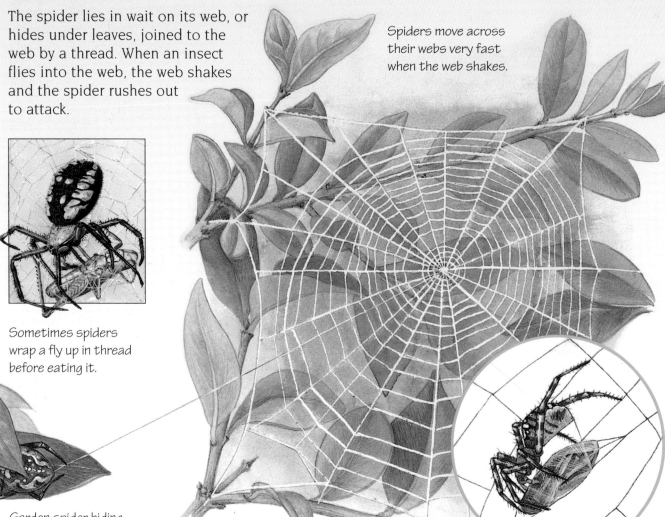

Sometimes spiders wrap a fly up in thread before eating it.

Garden spider hiding

### Sheet webs

House spiders spin sheet webs in the corners of rooms. Insects can't escape the fine threads.

### Tube webs

The wall spider spins a tube-like web in cracks in walls. It pulls unwary insects down into the tube.

### Nursery webs

One kind of wolf spider spins a web like a tent around her eggs. She tears it open when the baby spiders hatch.

### Money spiders

These tiny spiders spin fine webs like hammocks across a lawn. The webs sometimes blow away in the wind.

## Web sketches

Go on a web hunt one fall morning and make sketches of them. Look carefully at them but do not touch them as you will break the fine threads.

### You will need
Sheets of black paper or cardboard
A fine silver felt pen or gel pen

**1.** First draw the framework of the web that runs around the outside. Then add the spokes that go into the middle.

**2.** Next draw the inside pattern. If it is a spiral, start in the middle and work carefully out to the edge.

*No two webs look exactly the same.*

# Planting bulbs

Many spring flowers grow from bulbs, but you have to plant them in the fall, 8 to 12 weeks beforehand. You can plant them in a garden, or in pots. You can also plant them in indoor pots, as long as you keep them in a cool, dark place for two to three months. Indoor bulbs flower earlier than outdoor ones because it is warmer inside.

Crocuses

Daffodils

### You will need

A large, frost-proof pot with drainage holes in the bottom
Gravel or pebbles
Potting compost or bulb fiber
Bulbs, such as narcissi, tulips, crocuses or dwarf irises
A stick

## Outdoor pots

**1.** Put a layer of gravel in the pot, then fill two thirds of it with compost. Make a hole for each bulb.

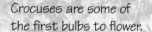

*Crocuses are some of the first bulbs to flower.*

**2.** Put each bulb in a hole with the pointed end facing upward. The bulbs must not touch each other.

**3.** Fill the pot with compost so the bulbs are buried twice as deep as their own height. Put the pots outside.

# Growing bulbs indoors

Good indoor bulbs are hyacinths, amaryllis, dwarf irises and narcissi, such as "Paper white" and "Tête-à-tête". Plant hyacinths early in the fall to flower in the winter.

A hyacinth flowers after 12-15 weeks.

**1.** Put gravel and bulb fiber or compost in a pot as above. Don't fill the pot to the top.

**2.** Gently press a bulb into the middle, pointed end up. Fill in compost around the edges.

**3.** Stand the pot on a saucer. Water the compost around the bulb, to make it moist.

**4.** Put the bulb in a cool, dark place for 8 to 10 weeks. Keep the compost damp.

**5.** When the leaves have grown as tall as your first finger, stand the pot in a light, cool place.

**6.** When the plant has grown a little more, put it in a warm, light place and a flower will grow.

## Growing hyacinths in water

You can also grow hyacinths in water, without any soil, and watch their roots and leaves grow. You can either grow them in a special hyacinth jar, or suspended in a jar with toothpicks. It is best to wear gloves when you handle the bulbs, as they can give you a rash.

### You will need
Rubber gloves or old gloves
A hyacinth bulb
3 toothpicks
A glass jar or hyacinth jar

Special hyacinth jar

**1.** Fill the jar almost full with cold water. Wearing gloves, push the toothpicks into the fattest part of the bulb.

**2.** Rest the toothpicks on the rim of the jar, so that the fat end of the bulb is just above the water.

**3.** Put the jar in a cool, dark place. Once the roots have grown, move it to a warm, light place.

# Chocolate cobweb cake

Make this delicious cake for a fall party or celebration. It is very easy because all the ingredients are mixed together in the same bowl. Remember to allow time for the cake to cool before you ice it.

## You will need

For the cake:
2 rounded tablespoons cocoa
4 tablespoons hot water
1 cup soft margarine
1 cup sugar
4 eggs
1 ¾ cups self-rising flour
1 level teaspoon baking powder

Two 8-inch round pans

For the frosting:
8oz. semi-sweet baking chocolate
½ cup butter
2oz. white chocolate

Oven temperature: 350°F

## Making the cake

**1.** Set the oven. Grease the two cake pans and line both with a circle of greaseproof paper.

**2.** Put the cocoa in a bowl. Slowly stir in the hot water, to make a smooth paste.

**3.** Put all the other cake ingredients in a mixing bowl. Add the cocoa mixture then beat everything together well.

**4.** Pour half the mixture into each pan. Bake the cakes for 25-30 minutes, until they have risen and are firm.

The cake is really chocolatey inside. It serves about 14 people.

**5.** Run a knife around the edges of the cakes, then turn them out onto a wire rack to cool.

## Icing the cake

**1.** Put the semi-sweet chocolate into a small bowl. Stand it over a pan of water over a low heat.

**2.** Cut up the butter and add it to the bowl. Stir the butter and chocolate until they have melted.

**3.** Sandwich the cakes together with half of the icing. Spread the rest over the top and sides.

**4.** Break the white chocolate into a bowl. Stand it over a pan of hot water and stir it until it melts.

**5.** Let the chocolate cool for five minutes. Spoon the chocolate into one small plastic bag inside another.

**6.** Hold the bag over a plate and snip off a tiny corner. Be careful not to let the chocolate run out.

*Use dark and white chocolate to make patterns in the frosting.*

**7.** Gently squeeze the bag to draw a circle on top of the cake. Draw more circles around it.

**8.** Pull the tip of a knife from the center of the cake to the edge several times to make a pattern.

## Serving the cake

Once you have iced the cake, leave it for a while to let the icing set before serving it. The cake tastes best the day you make it, but it will keep for several days as long as you keep it in an airtight container.

*You can make a different pattern by piping lines across the cake and then dragging the tip of a knife across them.*

# Wildlife on the move

As the days grow shorter and colder in the fall, some birds and animals leave their summer homes and travel great distances to spend the winter in warmer lands where there is plenty of food. This is called migration. In spring, they return to their breeding grounds.

In the fall, Arctic terns fly from the Arctic all the way to the Antarctic, at the other end of the world.

## A long march

Reindeer and caribou live in the far North, near the Arctic Circle. In the winter, it is hard for them to reach the plants they eat buried beneath the snow and ice, so enormous herds of animals travel thousands of miles south in search of food. If they didn't do this, many of them would die.

A line of migrating caribou may stretch for 186 miles (300km ). Caribou are good swimmers so they can cross rivers on the way.

Monarch butterflies settle down to roost when the temperature drops below a certain level. These are on a tree trunk.

Monarch butterfly

## Butterfly travelers

Most butterflies don't survive the winter, but some of them migrate to warmer countries. In the fall, thousands of Monarch butterflies flock together and set off on an epic journey from Canada all the way to the Gulf of Mexico.

Birds that fly in flocks often have striking markings that help the rest of the flock to recognize them.

## Migrating birds

At the end of the summer, huge flocks of swallows gather on overhead wires before taking off on flights of 6,000 miles (9,700km) from Europe to southern Africa. Swallows eat insects, which are only plentiful in the spring and summer.

Swallow

Caribou follow the same migration routes every year. They can walk across deep snow because their wide hooves are fringed with fur, like snow-shoes.

Swallows have to fly all the way across the Sahara Desert on their journey south. There is hardly any water in the desert, so they fly non-stop. They live on food and water stored as fat under their skin.

Hoopoes fly from Europe to Africa every fall.

## Finding the way

Nobody is entirely sure exactly how birds find their way over such long distances. Birds that fly in the daytime may follow landmarks, such as rivers and mountains, or may find their way by the position of the Sun. Birds that fly at night may use the stars and moon to help them navigate.

# Preparing for winter

In the fall, wherever you live, you may find signs of birds and animals getting ready for the winter. Many of them stock up on food before it becomes scarce; others are preparing shelters or homes to keep them warm and safe for the winter.

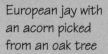

European jay with an acorn picked from an oak tree

## Storing food

In the fall, jays collect acorns from oak trees and bury them. They dig them up in the winter when they need food. Squirrels also bury nuts to eat later on in the winter. They eat seeds, cones and fruit too. They often have a favorite feeding place, such as a tree stump and scatter shells and leftovers around it.

Arctic fox in thick, white winter coat

## Winter coats

Many mammals, such as foxes, grow longer, thicker winter coats. This helps them to keep warm as the weather becomes colder.

Gray squirrel burying nuts in the fall. Any nuts that a squirrel forgets about may sprout and grow into trees.

## Wild corner

You can help animals find food and shelter for the winter by creating a wild corner in your backyard. Let the grass and weeds grow, to encourage insects and butterflies.

Fungi and mosses grow on rotten wood. Insects live in it, providing extra food for birds.

Leave fallen fruit for birds and animals to feed on.

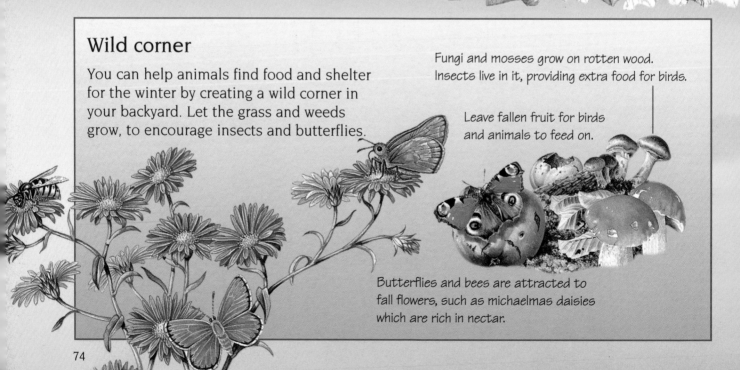

Butterflies and bees are attracted to fall flowers, such as michaelmas daisies which are rich in nectar.

# Winter

# The winter sky at night

These star maps will help you identify the constellations that you can see in the night sky in winter. The best time to use the maps is at around 11pm on a clear night, away from city lights.

## Maps for northern half of world

Facing north, look for Ursa Major balancing on its tail and Cygnus (the Swan). Looking south, winter is the best time to see Orion, one of the brightest constellations, high in the night sky. Orion contains several brilliant stars, including Betelgeuse, which is reddish in color, and Rigel, which is blue-white.

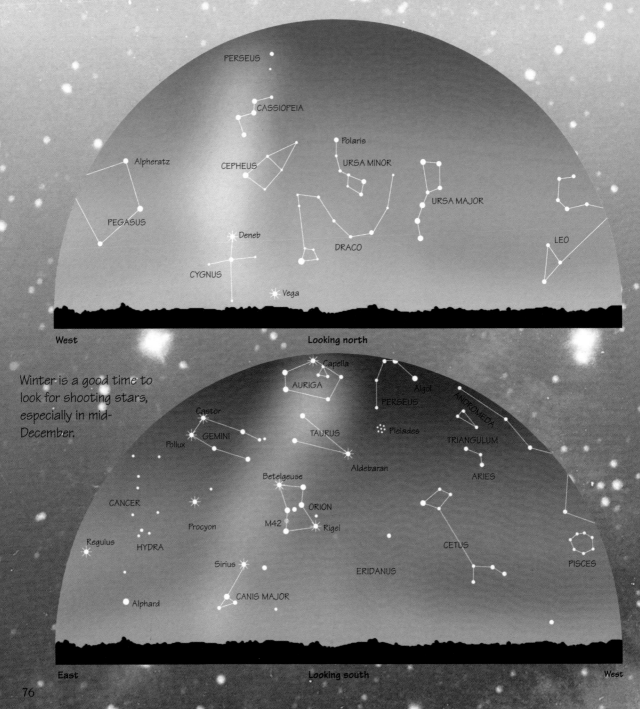

Winter is a good time to look for shooting stars, especially in mid-December.

# Maps for southern half of world

There are plenty of bright stars to look for at this time of year. Try to spot Deneb, Arcturus, Spica, Altair, Vega and Fomalhaut. Looking north, the easiest constellations to spot at this time of the year are Aquila (the Eagle),

Capricornus (the Sea Goat) and Sagittarius (the Archer). The Milky Way is seen at its best here, cutting the sky in half. Looking south, it runs through Crux (the Southern Cross) and Centaurus (the Centaur).

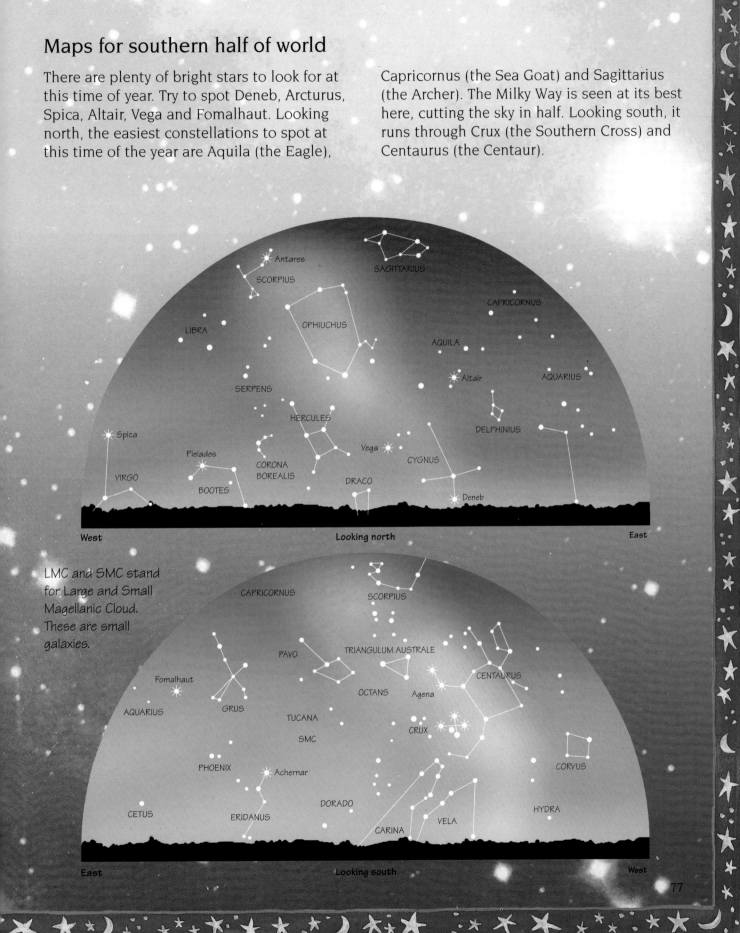

Antares
SCORPIUS
SAGITTARIUS
CAPRICORNUS
LIBRA
OPHIUCHUS
AQUILA
AQUARIUS
Altair
SERPENS
DELPHINIUS
HERCULES
Spica
Vega
Pleiades
CYGNUS
CORONA BOREALIS
VIRGO
DRACO
BOOTES
Deneb

West          Looking north          East

LMC and SMC stand for Large and Small Magellanic Cloud. These are small galaxies.

CAPRICORNUS
SCORPIUS
PAVO
TRIANGULUM AUSTRALE
Fomalhaut
CENTAURUS
OCTANS          Agena
AQUARIUS          GRUS
TUCANA
CRUX
SMC
PHOENIX          Achernar
CORVUS
CETUS          ERIDANUS          DORADO          VELA          HYDRA
CARINA

East          Looking south          West

77

# Winter weather

In most parts of the world, winter is colder than the other seasons. The days are also shorter and the nights longer. In countries where the temperature drops below freezing point for much of the winter, there is a lot of frost and snow. In some places there may be snow on the ground for several months.

Icicles form when it is so cold that drips of melting snow freeze.

Every snowflake is different but they all have six points.

## Frost

On cold, dry winter's nights there is often a frost. Freezing cold surfaces are covered with a fine layer of ice crystals. Rime is white frost that forms when an icy wind blows over grass and trees. Each branch and blade of grass is coated with a furry layer of ice crystals.

## Snow

When it is very cold, it may snow. The tiny drops of water in clouds freeze into ice crystals that join together to make snowflakes and flutter to the ground. For snow to settle, it has to be cold enough for it not to melt once it reaches the ground. Snowflakes are so small you can only see them properly under a microscope.

If you live in an area where it snows, you can make a snowman.

# Snowshaker

Make a model snowman inside a jar,
then shake it to create your own snowstorm.

## You will need
White, brown, red and green modeling clay
Silver glitter
A jar with a screw-top lid
Thin silver wire
Glycerin (available at a pharmacy)
Blue food coloring

**1.** Make a snowman on a mound out of the clay. It must be small enough to fit inside the jar.

**2.** Push the model snowman firmly onto the inside of the jar lid, so that it sticks in place.

**3.** Twist a piece of thin wire into a bare tree shape. Stick it into the "snow" next to the snowman.

**4.** Half fill the jar with glycerin. Pour in enough water to make the jar three-quarters full.

**5.** Pour quite a bit of silver glitter into the jar, then add a couple of drops of blue food coloring.

**6.** Lower the model slowly into the jar. The liquid will rise to fill the jar. Screw the lid on tightly.

Shake the shaker to make it snow. The glycerin in the water helps make the snow fall gently.

**7.** Dry the outside of the jar, then turn it right-side up and watch the snow flutter down.

You can use any model that the water won't spoil. This is a model of a house on a hill.

# Stormy skies

Watercolors are very good for painting moody skies and clouds, especially if you wet the paper first. Before you start a picture, try some of the ideas shown below to find out how to create different effects. You only need three colors for the picture. It's a good idea to try mixing them first, to see how many different colors you can make.

You can buy watercolors in tubes or pans.

## You will need
Watercolor paints
A thick paintbrush
A small sponge
Tissues
Watercolor paper
A plate or palette

Mix yellow and blue to make green.

## Mixing greens

Mix yellow and blue together. Then mix in small amounts of burnt umber to make different shades of green.

## A thundery sky

Wet the paper. Paint a wash of mid blue (see page 14), then paint a wash of dark blue over the top half of it.

## Painting clouds

**1.** Wet the paper and paint a blue wash over it. To make clouds, dab off patches of paint with a tissue.

**2.** If you want to make the clouds look like rain clouds, add a darker color along the bottom of each cloud.

As a finishing touch, you could add some flying birds to your stormy sky painting.

## Stormy sky picture

You will need to use three different watercolor paints for this stormy sky picture: Prussian blue, yellow ocher and burnt umber. If you don't have these colors, use whichever shades of dark blue, yellow and brown that you do have.

**1.** Wet a sheet of watercolor paper all over, using the small sponge or thick paintbrush.

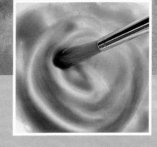

**2.** On your palette or plate, mix Prussian blue with burnt umber to make dark gray.

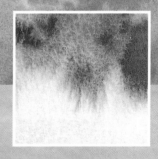

**3.** Dab large patches of dark gray paint onto the top part of the paper with your paintbrush.

**4.** Clean your brush, then add patches of yellow ocher to the dark gray, so they run together.

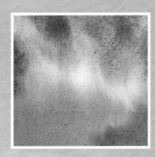

**5.** Mix three or four different shades of green and dab them over the bottom part of the paper.

**6.** Build up the patches of green so they run into the gray paint, to create a rainy effect.

**7.** When the sky has dried, paint a castle with the same dark gray paint you used for the clouds.

# Winter buds

In the winter, trees hardly grow at all, but slow down and rest. Most broadleaved trees have no leaves in winter, but they all have buds containing the baby leaves, shoots and flowers for the coming spring. The winter buds and twigs of different trees may look different, but they all have the same basic features.

## Winter twigs

On the right is a three-year-old horse chestnut twig. Its buds have sticky scales. They grow opposite each other in pairs. The leading bud holds next year's shoot. It is covered with thick scales that protect it from the cold and insects. The new stem and leaves are inside the scales.

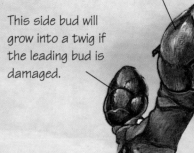

Leading bud

This side bud will grow into a twig if the leading bud is damaged.

A leaf scar left by last year's leaf

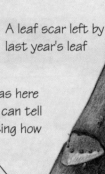

Last year's leading bud was here and left a girdle scar. You can tell how old a twig is by counting how many girdle scars it has.

This side shoot grew from a side bud. It is two years old.

These side buds will grow into leaves.

Leading bud

Last year's buds were here.

The twig above is from a two-year-old Norway spruce. The spruce is an evergreen, so it does not lose its leaves each winter.

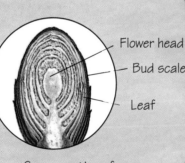

Flower head

Bud scales

Leaf

Cross-section of a horse chestnut bud

Horse-chestnut sticky buds

## Forcing buds

You can 'force' some buds to open in the winter, sooner than usual, by cutting some twigs and bringing them indoors. Some twigs to try forcing are forsythia, horse chestnut, birch and willow. Stand the twigs in a vase or glass jar in a sunny spot, then wait for the buds to open.

# Spotting winter buds

If you look carefully at winter buds and twigs, you can spot the differences between them. This will help you identify which tree they come from. Check to see if the buds grow in opposite pairs, or singly - first one side of the twig then the other. Look at their color and shape. Are the buds covered with scales or furry hairs? If there are scales, how many and are they sticky? Here are some different twigs you might see.

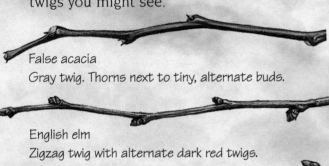

**False acacia**
Gray twig. Thorns next to tiny, alternate buds.

**English elm**
Zigzag twig with alternate dark red twigs.

**Common lime**
Zigzag twig. Alternate, reddish buds with two scales.

**Walnut**
Thick, hollow twig. Big, black alternate buds.

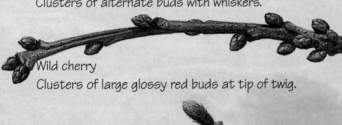

**Turkey oak**
Clusters of alternate buds with whiskers.

**Wild cherry**
Clusters of large glossy red buds at tip of twig.

**Magnolia**
Huge, furry, greenish-gray buds.

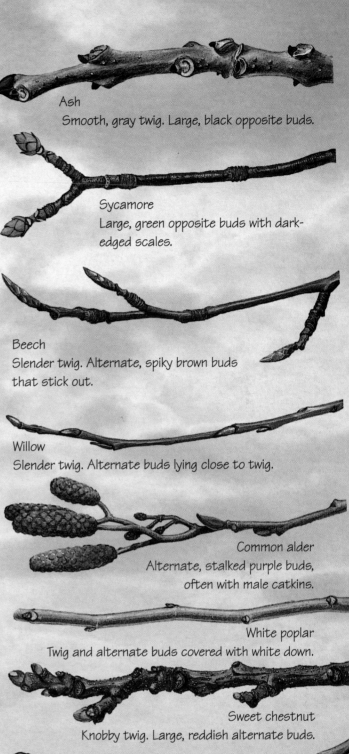

**Ash**
Smooth, gray twig. Large, black opposite buds.

**Sycamore**
Large, green opposite buds with dark-edged scales.

**Beech**
Slender twig. Alternate, spiky brown buds that stick out.

**Willow**
Slender twig. Alternate buds lying close to twig.

**Common alder**
Alternate, stalked purple buds, often with male catkins.

**White poplar**
Twig and alternate buds covered with white down.

**Sweet chestnut**
Knobby twig. Large, reddish alternate buds.

**London plane**
Alternate, cone-shaped buds. Ring scar around bud.

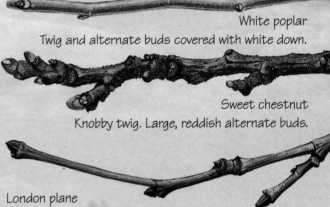

**Whitebeam**
Downy, green alternate buds.

# Winter trees

Each type of tree has its own special shape, depending on the shape and size of its trunk and the way its branches grow. You can see the shapes of trees best in the winter, when many of them lose their leaves. This gives you a good chance to see their branches properly.

## Deciduous trees

Trees that lose their leaves in winter are called deciduous trees. Almost all of them have broad, flat leaves. Deciduous trees lose their leaves each fall, then grow new ones the following spring.

Copper beech

Horse chestnut

Field maple

English oak

## Evergreen trees

Evergreen trees keep their leaves all the year round. Most of them have long, thin leaves called needles, which have a hard, waxy surface. Some of them have tiny scale-like leaves that overlap each other.

Silver birch trunks

Corsican pine

Norway spruce

Blue Atlas cedar

Lawson cypress

# Tree spotting

Look for different trees when you are out in a park or the countryside in winter. Making quick sketches will help you remember what they look like. When you get home, compare your sketches with the pictures here, or look them up in a book.

Hawthorn

London plane

Monkey puzzle
(Chile pine)

Horse chestnut

Judas tree

## Looking at bark

Another way to recognize winter trees is to look at their bark. This is the tough outer layer of the trunk that protects a tree from disease. When a tree is young, its bark is smooth and thin. As the tree grows older, its bark gets thicker and forms different patterns.

Silver birch bark peels off in strips that look like ribbons or wood shavings.

The bark of an English oak tree has deep ridges and cracks.

A beech tree has smooth, thin bark that flakes off in tiny pieces.

The bark of the Scots pine flakes off in large pieces.

# Winter flowers

Few plants flower in the winter, because frost and ice harm them. But toward the end of the winter, when it starts to get warmer, the first flowers appear. Look for them in sheltered spots in gardens, parks or woodlands.

*Snowdrop*

*Christmas rose*

## The first flowers

Clumps of snowdrops with their tiny nodding flowers appear in late winter once any snow has melted. They grow from tiny bulbs.

*Winter aconite*

Winter aconites grow in sheltered flower beds and under trees. The small, yellow flowers appear in the late winter and early spring.

Christmas roses flower in the middle of winter, in shady, frost-free spots. The plant has dark, waxy evergreen leaves which can stand the winter cold.

Winter squills can be found in rock gardens at the end of the winter. The green leaves appear first, followed by the blue, bell-like flowers.

*Winter squill*

*Glory of the snow*

*Pasque flowers are bell-shaped.*

*Crocus*

Glory of the snow have small, star-shaped blue and white flowers. They grow in flower beds and rock gardens. The flowers open when the winter snow is melting.

Pasque flowers and crocuses come out at the end of the winter. The flowers only open when it is warm and sunny. If the sun goes in, they close their petals. You can find yellow and white crocuses as well as purple ones. Each color flowers at a slightly different time.

## Winter-flowering shrubs

At the end of the winter, these shrubs flower in sheltered places, adding a burst of color to the wintry landscape.

Winter jasmine (below) is often trained to grow up walls. The yellow trumpet-shaped flowers appear first, followed by small, glossy leaves.

Winter jasmine

Viburnam tinus

## Catkins

Some trees have two kinds of flowers that appear late in the winter in places with a mild climate. One kind of flower is female and makes seeds. The other type is male and makes pollen. The male flowers are called catkins and grow in clusters on long stalks.

Female flowers

Leaf bud

These male flowers make pollen. Lots of them grow together on a long stalk called a catkin.

Catkins come out in late winter or early spring before the leaves open. The wind blows them around and the pollen drifts away on the breeze.

Stamens that make pollen

Viburnum tinus is a bushy evergreen shrub with pointed oval leaves. The heads of pinkish-white flowers have a sweet smell.

Exotic camellia flowers appear at the end of the winter. The flowers can be red, pink or white and grow on shrubs with dark, glossy leaves. Camellia flowers can be damaged by frost, so they only grow well in mild, frost-free places.

Look for camellias in woodland and city gardens.

# Baked potatoes

Baked potatoes are one of the easiest things to cook and make a warming meal on a winter's day. Below are two suggestions for different fillings - tuna and sweet corn or cheese and bacon, but you can use any filling you like. The quantities given for the fillings here are both enough to fill two potatoes. Set the oven at least 20 minutes before cooking the potatoes, to give it enough time to warm up.

## You will need
2 large baking potatoes
Cooking oil
Butter or margarine

For the tuna filling:
6oz can tuna
1 tablespoon mayonnaise
7oz can sweet corn

For the cheese filling:
¼ cup cheese
2 tablespoons bacon topping

Oven temperature: 400°F

**1.** Set the oven. Hold the potatoes under running cold water and scrub them clean with a small brush.

**2.** Prick the potatoes all over with a fork. Rub them with cooking oil and put them on a cookie sheet.

**3.** Put the tray of potatoes on the top shelf of the oven. Cook them for an hour, then take them out.

**4.** Test the potatoes with a small knife to see if they are cooked. They should feel soft all the way through.

**5.** If still hard, cook them for another 15 minutes, then test them again. If they are soft, cut them in half.

**6.** Put a little butter or margarine into each potato. Then spoon in the filling you have chosen.

Baked potatoes filled
with tuna and sweetcorn
(left) and cheese (right)

## Tuna and sweetcorn filling

Pile the filling
onto the potato.

**1.** Open the cans of tuna and sweetcorn with a can opener. You may need to ask an adult to help you.

**2.** Drain the liquid from each can by holding down the lid and tipping it upside down over the sink.

**3.** Put the drained tuna into a small bowl. Mix in the mayonnaise and two tablespoons of sweetcorn.

## Cheese and bacon

Try fillings of butter,
or sour cream
and chives.

Grate the cheese onto a plate. Put half the cheese in each potato, then spoon a little bacon on top.

# Birdwatching

It is hard for birds to find enough to eat in the winter, so you can help them by putting out food and water for them in your yard or on a window ledge. This gives you a good opportunity to watch them at close hand.

Meadowlark

## Putting out food

These are foods that different birds like to eat. You can also buy wild birdseed from pet stores. Don't feed the birds in the breeding season in spring, as baby birds need natural food, such as insects and grubs.

Bread

Cheese

Bacon

Banana

Dried fruit

Cooked potato

| Food chart | | | |
|---|---|---|---|
| | WORMS | SNAILS | INSECTS |
| Blackbird | | | |
| Song thrush | | | |
| Robin | | | |

Scatter food on the ground for birds such as thrushes and blackbirds.

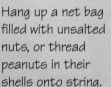

Hang up a net bag filled with unsalted nuts, or thread peanuts in their shells onto string.

To find out which foods birds like, make a chart showing what different birds eat.

Make a bird bath so the birds have water to drink and wash in. Change the water every day to keep it clean.

If you have a bird table, scatter food on the table and hang nuts or bird treats from hooks around the edges.

## Feeding time

Watch birds quietly, without disturbing them. Make notes of what they look like, or do quick sketches, to help you identify what they are.

## Making bird treats

### You will need
A yogurt container
String
A big needle
Cooking fat
Breadcrumbs, oats and cooked potato

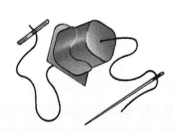

**1.** Thread the yogurt container onto the string. Fill it with the cooked potato, oats and breadcrumbs.

**2.** Ask an adult to melt the fat. Pour it into the yogurt container and mix in everything else.

**3.** Leave the fat to harden. Then hang the container upside down from the piece of string.

## Plants for birds

The plants shown below attract birds to a yard because they provide food. Shrubs and trees that produce berries in the fall such as rowan, crab apple, elder, and holly, are valuable sources of natural food for many birds.

Rowan

Groundsel

Hawthorn

Wild grasses

Cotoneaster

Elder

Thistle

Female bullfinch on sunflower seedhead

Blackbird on ivy

Do not cut the seed heads off teasles, sunflowers and thistles in the winter as finches and other birds will feed on any seeds that are left. You can also put sunflower seeds out on your bird table.

Ivy climbs up walls and trees and is used as a nesting site by many birds. Its berries provide food in the winter.

A blue tit drinking water from a dripping garden faucet

# Surviving the winter

Different animals have different ways of coping with the cold weather and lack of food in winter. Some of them go to sleep or hibernate all winter until spring comes. Others have thick coats to keep them warm, so they can continue looking for food throughout the winter.

Bats hibernate in hollow trees, caves or lofts. They sleep hanging from their claws, upside down.

## The big sleep

Some animals stock up on food during the fall, so they are well fed at the start of the winter. Then they burrow into their shelters and fall fast asleep. They don't eat all winter long. By the time spring comes, they are much thinner and need to find food.

Alpine marmot

## Alpine marmots

Alpine marmots seal themselves into their burrows under the ground and sleep for the winter, that is, for six months of the year. When they are asleep, their body temperature drops and their heartbeat slows down so they can survive until the spring without food.

Hedgehogs curl up in a ball and hibernate for five months in a nest of grass, moss and leaves.

Entrance blocked with earth and stones

Marmots hibernating

Chamber for droppings

## Winter in the den

Bears do not hibernate, as their bodies do not slow down in the winter, but they shelter in their dens

Hole for air

Main chamber

Cubs' chamber

Entrance tunnel

Some dens have a lower chamber too.

and doze. Female polar bears give birth to up to three cubs at a time in dens in the snow, where they are safe from the freezing winds outside. The cubs stay in the den for about three months, feeding on their mother's milk. The mother eats nothing herself. She just rests.

## Changing coats

Many Arctic and mountain animals which don't hibernate change the color of their coats at different times of the year. In the winter, their coats or feathers are white, making it hard to see them against the snow. In the summer, when the snow has melted, their coats are gray or brown, so they blend in with the surrounding rocks and plants. This camouflage makes it hard for both hunters and prey to see each other.

Arctic fox in winter coat

Snowshoe hare in winter coat

Snowshoe hare in summer coat

Arctic fox in summer coat

Ptarmigan in summer

Ptarmigan in winter

## Hibernating insects

Some insects spend the winter in hiding places, without moving or feeding. You may find them on tree trunks, under stones, in the corners of houses and sheds, in wood piles or among dead leaves. Note where you find them, but do not disturb them.

Moths often rest on bark of tree trunks, especially if they are the same color as the bark. Look in cracks in the bark and you may find pupae.

Green lacewing

Peacock butterfly

If you search the dusty corners of a shed in winter, you may be able to find a butterfly or a lacewing hibernating.

Above you can see some of the many different insects that like to hibernate in sheltered spots such as woodpiles in the winter.

# Useful information

## Equipment

You don't need special equipment or materials for most of the activities in this book, but there are some things you might find useful.

## Watching animals

For many of the nature activities in this book it is a good idea to have a pair of binoculars and a hand lens or magnifying glass. A good pair of binoculars when you are starting out is either 8x30 or 8x40 (The numbers tell you how strong and what size the binoculars are). Make sure they are light and comfortable to hold and ask an adult to show you how to focus them.

Other things that may be useful for watching animals are a notebook and pencil (for doing quick sketches or making notes), plastic bags and containers for collecting things, a small camera, string, labels and a small backpack to carry everything in.

## Gardening things

Go to a garden center or a big grocery store with a gardening section to buy everything you need for gardening, such as plant pots, potting compost, bulbs and seeds. Ask for help if you can't find what you want. The backs of seed packets give you all the information you need for planting seeds. Bulbs are usually only available in late summer and early fall, just before you should plant them.

## Art equipment

You can buy watercolor paints, pastels, pencils, paintbrushes, different sorts of paper and craft materials at your local discount retailers, or craft and hobby store. Look for boxes of paints and pastels that are specially made for children, as they are usually cheaper. Watercolor blocks are more economical to use than tubes. You don't need to buy a proper palette to mix paints. You can just use an old plate, or the lid from a plastic container.

---

## Taking care of nature

When you go for a walk or take part in a nature activity, take care of the countryside and its wildlife and make sure you stay safe.

- Always tell your parents or guardian where you are going and what you plan to do.

- Do not drop litter. Take your trash home with you.

- Keep to paths and close gates behind you.

- Leave things in the wild as you found them. Do not damage any plants or trees.

- When collecting things, only take what you need and make sure you leave plenty of specimens behind.

- Never disturb nesting birds or take birds' eggs.

- Be gentle with any creatures you catch, however small. Study them gently then put them back where you found them.

- Only pick wild flowers if there are plenty growing and only pick a few. Never uproot a plant or pick rare flowers.

## Activity tips

- Before you start, cover your work table with newspaper, unless you can wipe it clean. Put on an apron or old shirt and roll up your sleeves.

- Read the instructions before you start and gather everything together that you need.

- Be very careful with sharp knives and scissors.

- Never use a stove unless there is an adult there to help you.

- When cooking, wear oven gloves when picking up or moving any hot dishes or pans.

- When you have finished, clean up any mess you have made.

## Finding out more

If you want to find out more about animals and plants, write to the following organizations. Some of them have special wildlife clubs and magazines for children.

National Wildlife Federation
8925 Leesburg Pike
Vienna, VA 22184-0002 USA
Web site: www.nwf.org/nwf/index.html/

Wildlife Conservation Society;
2300 Southern Boulevard
Bronx, NY 10460-1099 USA
Web site: www.wcs.org/

American Birding Association
PO Box 6599
Colorado Springs CO 80934, USA
Web site: www.americanbirding.org/

Rainforest Action Network,
221 Pine Street
Suite 500
San Francisco, CA 94104, USA
Web site: www.ran.org/ran/

American Society for the Prevention of Cruelty to Animals
424 East 92nd Street
New York, NY 10128, USA
Web site: www.aspca.org/

American Zoo and Aquarium Association;
8403 Colesville Rd
Suite 710
Silver Spring MD 20910, USA
Web site: www.aza.org/

## More Web sites to visit

Kids Ark: web.ukonline.co.uk/conker/

The Really Wild Show (BBC TV nature program): www.bbc.co.uk/reallywild/

All About Birds:
www.zoomschool.com/subjects/birds/

The sea and the sky:
www.seasky.org/sea.html/

Heavens above (information on skywatching):
www.heavens-above.com/

# Index

Every effort has been made to trace the copyright holders of the material in this book. If any rights have been omitted, the publishers offer to rectify this in any subsequent edition, following notification. The publishers are grateful to the following for permission to reproduce material:

Cover: Tree © Richard Hamilton Smith/CORBIS; p4: Black tail deer and young © Darrell Gulin/CORBIS; p5: Frost-covered trees © Digital Vision; p9: Chick and eggs © Stockbyte; p13: Clouds © Digital Vision; p13: Palm trees © Douglas Peebles/CORBIS; pp14-15: Tulip field © Digital Vision; p16: Painted Lady runner bean © Photos Horticultural; p24: Chick and eggs © Stockbyte; p26: Adult cottontail rabbit © W. Perry Conway/CORBIS; p27: Young eastern cottontail rabbit © Lynda Richardson/CORBIS; p28: Ducklings © Julie Habel/CORBIS; p29: Piglets © Julie Habel/CORBIS; p29: Fox cubs © Manfred Danegger/Still Pictures; p31: Sunflowers © Digital Vision; p34: Yellow tulips and shadows © Michael S. Yamashita/CORBIS; p35: Sundial © The Purcell Team/CORBIS; p50: Combine harvester © Julian Calder/CORBIS; Summer fruits © Michelle Garrett/CORBIS; p51: Fly agaric toadstools © Digital Vision; p60 and 61: Autumn leaves © CORBIS Digital Stock; p62 and 63: Autumn leaves © CORBIS Digital Stock; p64-65: Fly agaric toadstools © Digital Vision; p67: Spiders' webs © Uwe Walz/CORBIS; p75: Snowflake © Jim Zuckerman/CORBIS; p78: Snowman © Stockbyte, Icicles © CORBIS Digital Stock, Snowflakes © Jim Zuckerman/CORBIS; p82: Horse chestnut buds © Sally A. Morgan; Ecoscene/CORBIS; p84: Silver birch trees © CORBIS Digital Stock; p85: Snow scene © CORBIS Digital Stock; p86: Camellias © The Purcell Team/CORBIS; p91: Blue tit and ivy © John Watkins; Frank Lane Picture Agency/CORBIS; p92: Pipistrel bat hibernating in cave © Tim Wright/CORBIS; All background photographs © Digital Vision